HAVING TEA WITH
Jesus

REGINA STONE MATTHEWS

All Scripture quotations, unless otherwise indicated are taken from
the Holy Bible, New International Version®, NIV® Copyright
©1973, 1978, 1984, 2011 by Biblica, Inc.® Used by permission. All
rights reserved worldwide.

For my grandma, Hattie Oxendine Bell, who taught me the importance of having tea with Jesus. An extraordinary woman of courage and strength.
I love you, Grandma.
I miss you still. Until we meet again.

Contents

Introduction

BACK IN THE EARLY 1980S, I SAW A MOVIE ABOUT THE kidnapping of a child and the events that took place to find him. The movie although gut-wrenching ended on a happy note. But the thing that caught my eye came in the form of a tip offered up by an elderly lady who the police and detective on the case had written off as a nut job. Why? Because she said, *while having tea with Jesus,* she saw the child playing in her neighbor's backyard.

I remember chuckling because I'd been having tea with Jesus since I was a kid. I got it from my grandma who told me that *it's always good to pray every day, but now and then you just might need to sit a while and have tea with Jesus.* The thing is, like the elderly lady, I'm sure at some point during my childhood years anyone seeing me talking aloud to no one might think me a nut job or that I invented an imaginary friend. I can state without hesitation I had no imaginary friends. I might actually be a nut job, but that's okay.

In the movie, it turned out the detective should have listened to the elderly lady because she *had* seen the child in the backyard of the house right next door to her. Now people can make all sorts of claims as to this woman's state of mind. I, on the other hand, make no such claim because I understand the importance of having tea with Jesus. As a side note, the woman's eyesight looked to be quite impaired. I do not doubt during her tea time with Jesus He said, "See that little boy over there in the yard? It's the same little boy they've been talking about on the T.V. Why not give the police a call and let them know?" So she did. But they ignored her for far too many days. It could have ended tragically had it not been for that special time known as having tea with Jesus.

Throughout my life, I find that having tea with Jesus allows me to sit and listen to what He has to say. It allows me to reflect on where I am in my life. Important events or insignificant events, they all come together at the tea table. Decisions are made there. Personal things I share with Him I find He welcomes there. Even the problems of a child He hears. He answers my questions. He instructs me and counsels me.

Any time of the day or night is the perfect time to have tea with Jesus. He's always up for a chat. During our tea time together, I realize that His love for me is never-ending. I know there will be occasions when He must scold me, just like when we as parents must scold our children. I am His child and He is my Father, after all.

I've taken the liberty of writing about some of the times I've had tea with Jesus. Silly times when we've laughed together. Serious times when we've cried together. Yes, Jesus cries with us just like he laughs with us. Times when I've been scared or confused and didn't know what to do. Times when Jesus just listened. I hope you enjoy them. But more than that, I hope you get something out of these stories, and maybe you'll even start having tea with Jesus.

When I think of my grandma I'm reminded of her wisdom. Her way of explaining things to me. All that time and since, I've cherished those moments when I sat and had tea with Jesus. And to this day I've remembered my grandma's words, because we all know there's always going to be "that time…"

HAVING TEA WITH
Jesus

1

That Time I Told My Mother to Shut Up

Ephesians 6:2-3

THERE ARE TIMES IN OUR LIVES WHEN WE DO THINGS AND THE moment we do them we know we've made a huge mistake. At the ripe old age of six, I made that mistake. That time, forever etched in my brain, reminds me of the importance of boundaries. One might think that being an only child means that child must be a brat. Not true in my case. My mother taught school before I came into her life. A disciplinarian from head to toe. She thought nothing of paddling my behind, hurting my feelings, or washing my mouth out with soap when needed. She also taught me a bucketful of important things I would need to know as I grew up.

I've written about my mother many times and referred to her as a character. But, then, so am I. We always had a different kind of relationship. She, always wanting me to do what she wanted me to do, and, me, always wanting to do what I wanted to do. That never worked well for either one of us. My antics seldom impressed her.

I'd just turned six years old that May in the year 1958. Turning six was a big deal for me, considering that my mother frequently told me I'd never live to be that old should I continue my current behavior. It amazes me to this day that I thought, on some level, that if I lived to the age of six it meant I could talk back to my mother without any fear of dying.

One must understand that six-year-old kids are just as dumb as sixteen-year-old teens. Something in the brain of kids at either age makes them feel invincible. I never thought of myself as a girly-girl, like my mother wanted. I loved climbing trees, playing marbles, riding bikes, and acting like a typical six-year-old tomboy. It drove my mother crazy. And that was the cherry on top of the cake. Making my mother crazy became my mission in life. Although when I did start noticing boys in that puppy love sort of way, my mother found it didn't make her feel any less troubled. She labeled me as boy-crazy. That always made me feel like I had a bit of an edge. The truth is that I was never *really* boy crazy to the extent she thought I might be. It just made my life happy making her believe that. But in her defense, I will state for the record that I did border on boy craziness.

For most of this six-year-old day, I'd been playing in the backyard with my friends. We always had the best time together, and this day was no different. Until…my mother called me in for supper. Now you must consider the year. In 1958, supper time meant every kid in every neighborhood, in every town, stopped playing when their mothers called them in for supper. It also meant family time. Being an only child didn't matter. Supper time brought an end to play.

As my friends began to scatter, I felt compelled *not* to go running home. I mean, I was six years old for crying out loud. The fact that my mother interrupted my playing held no weight with me. I stood my ground and giggled to myself at my dumb friends running the moment their mothers called them in for supper.

After about five minutes of me taking a stance against

tyranny, my mother called me again. This time her voice didn't seem as cheerful as the first time. In fact, it came across as quite perturbed. You see, mothers in the year 1958 would simply open the back door and yell for their kids to come inside. When the kid didn't come running and the mother called once more and still the kid didn't come, the mother would walk outside and stand in the yard. This meant a world of hurt would be coming that kid's way.

I saw my mother standing in the backyard—with her hands on her hips. Not a good sign at all. She called my name again, but this time she used all three of my names—Ellan Regina Stone! You know that look mothers give? Well, that look permeated my mother's face.

She said, "Did you hear me calling you?"

I just stood there, defiantly. To which my mother walked forward.

She then said, "When I call you in for supper, I expect to see you coming through that door. Now get inside!"

At that very moment, something evil came over me. I put my hands on my hips and without a thought in my head, I said, "Shut up!"

I don't remember what happened after that. All I know is that a whirlwind lifted me off the ground, and I found myself in my room without any supper and my backside burning. I knew at the time of this mishap that my making it to seven probably wouldn't happen.

That became the time I started having tea with Jesus. It's a conscience thing that God instills in us. It makes us know when we've done wrong. When we've been disrespectful to our parents. When we've been unkind to our friends.

The Bible tells us many times how we should treat our parents. "Honor your father and mother"—which is the first commandment with a promise— "so that it may go well with you and that you may enjoy long life on the earth." It not only tells us in Ephesians but also in twenty-two other books. That's a lot of instructions regarding the treatment of one's parents and elders. It would seem it's quite important to God that we understand this.

With the table set for tea and prayer, I bowed my head and closed my eyes. In my mind's eye, as I sat face-to-face having tea with Jesus for the first time, I remember He didn't coddle me. He called me out on my behavior, looking past my pitiful sad eyes yet loving me all along the way. As parents, we learn to do that same thing. I know this because after I'd spent some time in my room, my mother came in and talked with me about my behavior. From that moment on, I never told her to shut up again. That's not to say I magically became a perfect kid. It just meant I'd learned my lesson when it came to my mother's level of tolerance.

2

That Time I Got Lost in a Department Store

1 Peter 5:8

W E'VE ALL GOTTEN LOST AT ONE TIME OR ANOTHER IN our lives. It happens. Whether you are a wandering child or a wandering adult, getting lost is one of those things you experience. Sometimes it's being lost physically, and sometimes it's being lost mentally. It can be a learning experience or a scary one. That applies to kids as well as adults.

Looking back to that time I became lost in a department store, I realize it was neither a learning nor a scary experience. Why? Because when you are a wild and crazy kid, you simply don't learn or become scared by your actions. Why? Because you know your mother will find you and rescue you. And…you just don't care enough to be scared.

As a lover of wandering, especially in department stores, my mother often found me hiding among the racks of clothes. It's the best place to hide if you don't want to be seen. Since I always liked to hide there, it didn't take much time for my mother to find me. So I wasn't actually lost. I was simply wandering around and hiding. Sometimes my mother would play along and pretend to be concerned.

When she'd find me, she'd exclaim, "Oh my goodness! There you are! You scared me to death!" We'd laugh and that would be that. Shopping would continue.

Then one day, while in the department store, I wandered so far away that I became lost and it wasn't a pretend lost. When I realized this fact, it no longer seemed funny. Mother had turned her back to pay for her purchases. And although she'd told me to stay by her side, I took the opportunity to put a little spice into our department store visit by wandering farther away from her than usual.

As I frantically looked around for my mother, I remember thinking I'd never see her or my daddy ever again. Some monster with giant teeth and long sharp claws would jump out from among the racks of clothes and grab me, taking me off to parts unknown. The department store that seemed so familiar had become a gigantic arena with all sorts of frightening objects lurking around every corner.

I stood in the middle of nowhere that I could recognize and began to cry. Thankfully a kind soul took pity on me and helped me find my mother, who had not yet noticed I had disappeared. Naturally, when the good Samaritan tapped my mother on the shoulder to ask if this sobbing bundle of cuteness belonged to her, my mother looked down at me with the death stare. Every kid knows that stare. She thanked the kind stranger for rescuing me. But I knew once we got home, the sweet gratitude I heard in her voice would no longer be there.

Although this incident did not end my wandering, it did impress upon me the importance of making sure I could see my mother from every vantage point. A lesson I learned from Jesus as we sat that day in my room for quite a while and had tea together.

Isn't it odd that when we wander farther away than we intend, we end up becoming lost? I've become lost more times than I care to mention. And not just as a child. When we're lost, we become confused. We have trouble concentrating. Severe feelings of being lost can bring on hallucinations. Someone who is lost might become dizzy or nauseous. Their heart might beat faster, which could lead to them hyperventilating or experiencing shortness of breath. Heaviness in the throat or chest might occur. It's an all too scary feeling. It can, however, be a blessing.

Not unlike the lesson I learned from my department store adventure, as adults, we must make sure to keep our Father in Heaven in view from every vantage point during our wandering times. Peter speaks to this very thing as he reminds us "Be alert and of sober mind. Your enemy the devil prowls around like a roaring lion looking for someone to devour."

So the next time you decide to wander, be sure to follow Peter's advice. You might not be as lucky as I to be rescued by a good Samaritan before the lion gobbles you up.

3

That Time I Failed My Driver's Test

1 Corinthians 10:12

I LIVED IN ATLANTA, GEORGIA WHEN IT BECAME TIME FOR ME TO get my driver's license. I'd practiced driving with my daddy (an entirely different horror story) for an entire year. The year, 1968. With my student driving behind me, I felt more than ready to knock my driving test out of the park!

The morning of my driving test, I woke up at the crack of dawn. Totally unlike me. But this was the most important day of my life. Getting one's driver's license equaled independence. It meant you've arrived at that age where you no longer must depend on your parents to take you places. You now had the means to travel wherever you liked. No parental supervision.

As I ran downstairs, anxious to get to the DPS, my daddy met me with a big smile and asked, "Are you ready for this?"

Are you kidding me? I was born ready! I thought to myself.

I'd studied that driver's book for a year. My student driving teacher told me what an excellent driver I'd become, and he knew I'd pass that test with flying colors.

Traffic seemed to crawl as we made our way to the DPS.

The closer we got, I realized my palms were sweating. Wait a minute. Hadn't I just told Daddy I was born ready?

"You look nervous," my daddy said.

"Who me? Not me. I'm ready for this," I lied.

"Good. I know you're going to do just fine. Stay focused. Read each question on the written test carefully. Remember what you learned during student driving."

I appreciated Daddy's encouragement. It meant the world to me.

When we arrived at the DPS, I jumped out of the car, ready to take on the world. The clerk at the check-in desk was very nice. She handed me my test and wished me good luck. *Luck has nothing to do with it, honey. I've got skill and brain power.* I thought to myself. As I opened the test packet my confidence soared. I immediately knew the answer to the very first question. This was going to be a cake walk. It didn't take me very long to complete the test. An hour later they called my name to see the results of my written test. 100! I could hardly contain myself. I'm pretty sure I cracked a few windows screaming with joy.

Next came the driving test. Now that I'd aced the written test, the driving part would be no problem at all. Or so I thought. Overconfidence can ruin your day. What is overconfidence? Confidence that is not justified. Making yourself or your capabilities out to be more than you or they are.

My overconfidence story went like this:

Driving Examiner: Hello, Miss Stone. Are you ready to take your driving test? I see you made 100 on your written test. Congratulations.

Me: Hello! Yes, ma'am, I did. Thank you! I'm so ready!

Driving Examiner: Okay. Let's get started. Go ahead and crank the car and just follow the course.

Me. Yes ma'am! (To myself...*this is so easy*)

As I drove through the testing course, I knew, without a

doubt, that I would pass this test easily. I came to a complete stop at the various stop signs. I put on my blinker at the appropriate turns. I parked perfectly. Angle parking, perpendicular parking, and parallel parking. Had a photographer taken my picture at that moment, I'm sure my head would have grown ten inches. I even bet the photographer would put my photo in the DPS fliers. I all but had this test in the bag as I approached the final stop sign.

Driving Examiner: Continue to the front of the building.

Me: Yes ma'am. (Smiling broadly and not paying attention to the upcoming stop sign.)

Needless to say, I didn't stop at the stop sign. I drove right through it all the way to the front of the building.

Driving Examiner: I'm sorry Miss Stone. I'm going to have to fail you on your driving test. You didn't stop at that last stop sign. You can retake this part of the test in two weeks.

Me: What? I thought I did what you told me to do. To continue on to the front of the building.

Driving Examiner: Yes, I did say that. But it's your responsibility to know that you must always stop at a stop sign. I never said the test was over. Had you been on an actual road, you could have caused an accident. I'm sorry. You'll have to take the test again."

Mortified, I didn't know how I would ever be able to tell Daddy I'd failed the driving part of my test. Two weeks. I had to wait two weeks. That's a lifetime. Who made up these stupid rules anyway? To my surprise, Daddy didn't berate me, and his understanding of my error did a lot for my ego. He told me not to worry. We'd come back in two weeks, and I wouldn't make the same mistake next time.

When I got home, I went straight to my bedroom. I needed a good cry, and I needed to have tea with Jesus. It seemed all too tragic. We learn about overconfidence in 1 Corinthians. "So, if

you think you are standing firm, be careful that you don't fall!"
1 Corinthians 10:12

A hard fall, to be sure. But the lesson was well worth it. I went back to the DPS and passed the driving part of the test with a score of excellence. Tea with Jesus helped, as always. I tried to control my overconfidence in future years. Although I never had my own car as a teen, my parents allowed me to drive theirs whenever I wanted. I remembered that stop sign every time I drove their car. And to this day I can honestly say I've never gotten a ticket for rolling through a stop sign. I've never even gotten a ticket. That sound you hear is me knocking on wood!

4

That Time I Ran Away

Jonah 1:1-17

AS AN ONLY CHILD, YOU BEAR THE RESPONSIBILITY OF KNOWING if anything breaks in your house there are no other kids living there to blame it on. Things like your mother's favorite vase, your daddy's favorite fishing pole, the table lamp in the formal living room, and the massive toilet paper clogging the upstairs toilet that made it overflow. This was my life. The life of an only child.

Don't get me wrong, there are some benefits associated with being an only child. You get your own room. You don't have to share your toys. You can be alone whenever you want without having to deal with brothers or sisters. There are always plenty of snacks just for you. Your aunts and uncles spoil you rotten. It's pretty sweet, in those areas. It can also be very lonely at times.

I remember asking my parents why they wanted only one kid. They explained that they wanted more kids, but my mother had a miscarriage when I was two, and the doctor didn't recommend she try to have another baby. It made them very sad.

They said that's why they directed all their love toward me. It made me feel quite special.

So why, with this much love, would I run away? It all started with the bull.

When I was in elementary school, I didn't have to ride the bus, I could walk. I loved walking to school. It made me feel grown up. We didn't live very far away, and it didn't take me long to walk. Nevertheless, my mother always stood at the end of our driveway to make sure I made it halfway. That always annoyed me. It made me feel like a little kid for that part of the walk.

Each day, she warned me to stay on the sidewalk and not to cut across the fenced-in field that offered a bit of a short-cut to school. We all know that elementary school-aged kids know much more than their mothers. It's simply a fact. I knew of no reason why I couldn't cut through the field. If one day I might be running late, cutting through the field would save me some time.

One day I decided my mother just didn't know what she was talking about. What possible harm could come of cutting through the field? Even though I was on time, I thought I'd see how much time it would save if I crossed the field. I threw my book satchel over and proceeded to climb the fence. Safely on the ground, I picked up my satchel and began walking. What a feeling of liberty and freedom! I'd disobeyed my over protective mother. This would be a day I would write about in future years.

I hadn't gone fifty feet when I heard a strange noise. It sounded like heavy breathing. Being the kid who knew more than her mother, I never bothered to look around once I jumped the fence. I was on a mission of disobedience with no time to be bothered with the ridiculous safety rules my mother pounded into my head daily.

Suddenly, from nowhere, a bellowing bull running full speed came right toward me. I let out a blood-curdling scream, enough to break any window. Running as fast as I could with the bull hot on my heels, I reached the other side of the field, arms outstretched as I got closer to the fence. But not before the bull caught one of its horns in the seat of my pants. Fortunately, his horn caught me in mid-climb, and the only thing injured was my pride and my torn pants.

So much for knowing more than my mother!

I made it to school, but my troubles weren't over. Seeing my torn pants, my teacher, the tattletale, called my mother and snitched on me, not only about my pants, but my incident with the bull. She'd gotten that bit of information out of me through her relentless interrogation. As one might imagine, my mother was none too happy. She instructed my teacher to send me home immediately, knowing I'd never again cut through that field.

While on my way home, I debated running away. Kids did it all the time, I rationalized. Where would I go? I had no idea. I only knew if I went home, I'd be facing one of the biggest punishments known to kidhood. I'd probably never see my friends again. My bedroom would become my prison cell. They'd make me live on bread and water! I concluded I had no choice. I began walking in the opposite direction of my house.

When enough time had passed that I should have made it home, my mother drove my route to the school, looking for me. After talking with my teacher, my mother scoured the surrounding area. She finally found me walking down the sidewalk of a neighborhood several blocks away from the school. As I walked, head down, satchel hanging loosely from my fingertips, I imagined nightfall and how I would survive the dark. I began to cry. If only I'd listened to my mother.

My mother drove slowly beside me as I walked. I didn't noticed her since I was too busy feeling sorry for myself. Don't we all do that? Feel sorry for ourselves when we've done something wrong? Most times we know it's wrong when we're doing it. But we do it anyway. Then when the truth comes out, so does the self-pity.

I'm reminded of the story of Jonah and the whale. Jonah ran away, too. Except Jonah ran away from God and what He wanted Jonah to do. He didn't run away once. He ran several times. Every time he ran, he met misfortune, until a whale came along and swallowed him. That bull was my whale. "Now the Lord provided a huge fish to swallow Jonah, and Jonah was in the belly of the fish three days and three nights." Jonah 1:17.

As I walked down the sidewalk, I suddenly heard my mother's voice. "Regina. Where are you going?"

Startled, I looked up and saw my mother's face. No anger, no rage, no I told you so. She got out of the car and held out her arms. I ran to her, and she hugged me ever so tightly.

"I'm sorry," I said in a weepy voice.

"That's all I needed to hear," she replied. And as she picked me up, she kissed my cheek. I hugged her again. Tighter this time. We got in the car and drove home.

Tea with Jesus that night taught me many things. The wrongness of disobedience. The foolishness of running away. The importance of lessons and the joy of forgiveness.

5

That Time I Ran Off and Got Married

Genesis 2:24-25

A S A SENIOR IN HIGH SCHOOL, I MET A GUY WHO SWEPT ME off my feet. An athlete with a record-breaking high school career. Both in football and baseball. Scouts from both fields wanted him—especially baseball. Our senior year together as a couple played out like a Hallmark movie. Consequently, after we graduated from high school, we immediately began planning our future together as man and wife.

There was one little hiccup, however. That being my parents. They didn't approve of him and minced no words when expressing their thoughts. It infuriated me. I couldn't make them understand that this guy meant the world to me. He filled my heart to overflowing. His character, his talent, and his adoration of me proved that we were meant to be together. I couldn't understand why they couldn't see that. Why they couldn't see how much we loved each other. We both understood we were young, but hey, we both had friends who were getting married right out of high school. What was the problem? What could possibly go wrong?

Yet a problem existed, bubbling just below the surface. Our young eyes couldn't see it, but my parents' experienced eyes could. They told me in no uncertain terms that I must end this relationship at once. We argued nonstop for days. Me, crying buckets. My parents, warning me that this guy would bring nothing but misery should I continue this nonscience about marriage.

My acceptance letter into West Georgia College had arrived several weeks before graduation. I'd already toured the campus, picked out a dorm, and my daddy paid my first semester tuition and dorm fee. With all my classes scheduled, I knew I had no choice but to leave at the end of summer and check into my dorm. But regardless of the college plans, my guy and I knew we were going to get married.

My first semester went by like slow-running molasses. Each day seemed longer than the next. We exchanged letters almost every day. When Christmas break finally arrived, I begged my parents not to make me stop seeing him. I lied and made promises that we were no longer talking about marriage, when in fact our plot to marry was in the works. We would see as little of each other as possible over the holidays. That would convince my parents that we were all in agreement regarding our relationship.

At the end of my Christmas vacation, I returned to school with no intention of staying there. My guy waited outside my dorm until after my parents left. When they were nowhere in sight, I gave him the all-clear. We packed up his car with my suitcases and off we drove to South Carolina, where teens could get married without parental consent. A perfect plan.

We returned home the next day. Not to my home but his. His parents were more understanding than mine, and we thought it best to tell them first. They were none too happy but accepted it and offered an invitation to stay with them.

Terrified to tell my parents about our elopement, I took the coward's way out and wrote them a letter. Smacks of confidence in one's decision, yes?

When the letter arrived, my parents called to tell me they wanted to see me. Looking back on this now as a grown woman, mother of three daughters, and six grandchildren I'm sure my parents were devastated. I'm sure they were angry. I'm sure they literally wanted to strangle me as I stood in front of them. The disappointment in their faces ran over me like a Mack truck. I could hardly look at them. The scene didn't play out well. Yelling and crying ensued. It finally ended with an agreement that we couldn't change the situation. We'd simply have to live with it. I knew I could live with it. I'd married the love of my life—my soulmate. I didn't believe my parents would ever accept my marriage, much less live with it. In the end, I was the one who couldn't live with it.

Why do couples elope? Too many reasons to count. In my life, I learned that elopement should be the last option we choose. Grownups (also known as adults) are free to marry in any way they see fit. However, teens (also known as young people) should seek the approval of their parents. The Bible tells us to honor our parents. Should this not apply to those who want to marry? Should they not honor their parents by asking for their blessings—their approval? When a Christian couple marries, they leave their father and their mother and cling to one another. Like Genesis 2:24-25 reads; "That is why a man leaves his father and mother and is united to his wife, and they become one flesh. Adam and his wife were both naked, and they felt no shame."

The definition of eloping is to run away with one's lover and get married secretly, without any knowledge of the marriage or consent of the marriage by one's parents and/or family. Sadly, most young couples who choose elopement do so because they don't want to listen to their parents. Especially if their parents are Christians. As Christian parents, we see marriage through Godly eyes, with Godly wisdom. When young couples refuse to listen to that wisdom, a ton of heartache, as well as mistakes, can happen. It would be nice if we didn't have to learn these lessons the hard way.

Within a year of my young marriage, I became pregnant. I was 19. I turned 20 four months after her birth. By that time, my marriage had not turned out as I'd planned. The all-American athlete I thought to be my soul mate took on a new personality. His dreams of becoming a professional baseball player came to a sudden end when he threw his arm out during training camp for the Braves. The doctor said he could no longer play. Naturally, it hit him hard, which led to depression and then anger.

For the next three years, he would leave without a word, stay away for a few months, then return for a few months, vowing he wouldn't leave again. He never kept that vow. It happened over and over, until I couldn't take it any longer and filed for divorce. Raising our child in that type of environment would never work. I spent many evenings having tea with Jesus. He told me He would never leave me. That He would be right by my side every step of the way. He fulfilled His promise, and my little girl and I grew up together.

I never in a million years thought he would turn out as he did. That characteristic hidden just below the surface that I never saw. The divorce was ugly. I found myself raising and caring for my little girl alone. He had no time for her. When I remarried several years later, he called to say he didn't want to pay child support any longer. He wanted to give her up. My husband jumped at the chance to adopt her. We went through all the proceedings and, in the end, she grew up happy and healthy surrounded by people who loved her.

One day, many years later, I received a phone call from my

ex-husband. He apologized for all he'd put us through. By this time, I no longer carried that seed of hatred inside me. God had removed it long ago. I told him I no longer held any grudges and wished him well. Two weeks later, he died.

The call must have been his last confession. I discovered he'd been ill for quite some time. A life that could have turned out differently ended from the results of drug use.

We never forget our first love. Nevermind the struggle. I'll always remember him as a gifted athlete who made me laugh uncontrollably and who at one time in my life, I loved.

6

That Time I Hated God

Ephesians 4:26-27 / Proverbs 26:24-26

I WROTE ABOUT BEING ANGRY WITH GOD IN MY BOOK *ANYONE SEEN My Rose-colored Glasses?* published a few years back. The chapter "Remembering Will Have to Do" speaks of the passing of my Uncle Buck. who never had a chance to live out his life. I blamed God for this. Uncle Buck died in a horrific and senseless car accident at the age of thirty-six. It took me a long time to come to terms with his death. I shouted at God. I told Him I hated him.

I didn't.

Hating does nothing to the person you hate. It does everything to you. It eats you from the inside out. Hate should have no place in man or the world. Hate destroys. Hate is a rot that starts small then festers, growing larger and larger.

"Enemies disguise themselves with their lips, but in their hearts they harbor deceit. Though their speech is charming, do not believe them, for seven abominations fill their hearts. Their malice may be concealed by deception, but their wickedness will be exposed in the assembly." Proverbs 26:24-26

When my Uncle Buck died, it hollowed me out. I loved him

21

so much. I was fourteen at the time. The saddest of days for my family. At the time, I thought I hated God. It was really anger. Some might ask if it's okay to be angry with God. It is, as long as the anger doesn't last. "In your anger do not sin": Do not let the sun go down while you are still angry, and do not give the devil a foothold." Ephesians 4:26-27.

During that difficult time of thinking I hated God, I felt lost and empty. When I realized it was anger, the lost and empty feeling became less. I had to spend many tea times with Jesus to come to that conclusion. My grandpa (Uncle Buck's father) also helped me along the way, to understand the tragedy of it all and to make sense of it.

The loss of my Uncle Buck helped me to understand several things.

1. Tomorrow is never promised to anyone. That's why it's so very important to live each day as if it were your last. In such a hurried and complicated world, I get that's a difficult thing to do. I don't believe God expects us to always do it. But it's a great goal to reach toward.

2. Hate is never the answer to anything. It has no place in God's world.

3. God can handle us being angry with Him. However, the anger should never last very long. No good can come from it.

4. God is smarter than any person or people. Once we get that, we're better for it.

5. God never left me during the loss of my Uncle Buck. He stayed through all my tears and my anger.

6. Saying goodbye to my Uncle Buck was not a forever goodbye. We will see one another again in a much better place.

7. God understood my anger and loved me anyway. He

allowed me to get my anger out, because it meant I was talking with Him about the death of my Uncle Buck.

8. God has dealt with anger before. He dealt with Moses' anger. David felt abandoned by God and became angry. Job cried out to God and asked Him why He didn't answer him. Even Jesus asked God why He had forsaken Him.

9. My anger with God made me aware of His unconditional love for me.

10. We must ask for God's forgiveness for our anger and allow Him to heal our pain.

When I understood that God did not reach down from heaven and cause the accident that took my Uncle Buck's life, nor did God see it happening and simply let it happen, a peace came over me. God hears us, He loves us, He cries when we cry, He rejoices when we rejoice, and He knows our every need and emotion.

As I sat and had tea with Jesus in the days and months following that loss, Jesus reminded me of all the good times Uncle Buck and I shared throughout my fourteen years of life. He reminded me of the time Uncle Buck took me to the state fair and I wandered away from him and when he found me, he hugged me so tight I thought my ribs would break. All the times I visited with him, my grandma, and my papa. All the times he let me drive around with him in his car. And the time he picked me up in his arms and told me how much he loved me and how proud he was of me.

I miss Uncle Buck still and will love him forever and beyond. Until we meet again, remembering will have to do.

7

That Time I Saw My Daddy in ICU

Isaiah 43:2

I CAN'T REMEMBER A TIME IN MY LIFE WHEN I SAW MY DADDY tremble at the sight of anything. Daddy served our country for over twenty-five years. He fought in World War II and Korea. He began his career in the Army, first as a private, and ended his career as a Master Sergeant.

At the beginning of his career, he worked in the kitchen as a cook. Not because he sought out that position, but because he could cook like nobody's business. He never planned to stay there but soon worked his way to Sergeant—or should I say, Drill Sergeant. He trained many recruits throughout his military career. Tough as nails, they all said of him. Army through and through, they said. I simply replied, "He's my daddy."

Daddy was the strongest man I've ever known. Strong in mind, body, and soul. Never wavering in his positions. The words conviction, values, morals, and truth were words he lived by. No grey area. As a child, I thought him awe-inspiring. As a teen, I thought him stern and unyielding. As an adult, I discovered him human and fallible.

At the age of seventy-six, my superhuman daddy passed

away. He'd become frail and sickly. Bed ridden the last year of his life. His legs, his lungs, and his heart could no longer sustain him. In a last-ditched effort to show his strength, he got out of bed and walked to the rocking chair in the corner of the room. He hadn't walked in several months. He then got up from the rocking chair and walked to the bathroom where he collapsed, waking my mother who ran to his aide to no avail. I spent many hours having tea with Jesus in the days following.

Years prior, Daddy had open heart surgery. He came through it like the superman I knew him to be and went on to recover better than the doctors expected. I knew he wouldn't have had it any other way. He would never allow himself to show any weakness. We could hardly get him to stay put for any length of time. He just wanted the recuperation period to be over.

In April of 1982, I was pregnant with my third child. Well into my ninth month I received a call that Daddy had been admitted into the hospital. He was in ICU. He'd suffered what they thought to be a heart attack or possible stroke. They intubated him because he wasn't responding to meds and his breathing had become shallow.

When I arrived at the hospital and they showed me to his room, I remember thinking, *Daddy? Daddy this can't be you. You look so weak. You don't look like my daddy. My daddy is the strongest man I know. Daddy!*

At that point, he opened his eyes and looked at me. He could see the horror on my face. He tried to talk, but of course, the ventilator wouldn't allow it. I put my hand on his and he motioned with his other hand for the nurse to remove the ventilator. It broke my heart. I told him not to worry, that everything would be okay. He motioned once again, but this time at my large baby-filled belly. I told him all was good, and I knew he'd be around for the birth. The next morning, I went into labor.

Daddy recovered and spent the next several years as Papa to my girls. During that time, he spoiled them rotten, doting on them constantly. He insisted on taking my oldest daughter to dance and gymnastics. He taught my middle daughter how to bait a hook and where to find the best fishing holes and drove her to band practice. He taught my youngest daughter all about baseball and drove her to band practice too. Making himself available to all of us remained his top priority.

Daddy went to be with the Lord in 1995. I prayed diligently for him during his last days because I knew he'd felt betrayed by the church in years past. My mother put my fears to rest when she told me that Daddy told her he'd made peace with God. The burden I carried of the real possibility of not seeing my daddy in heaven fell off me and crashed to the ground, crumbling into millions of pieces. That night when I heard of Daddy's passing, having tea with Jesus reassured me that Daddy had found his way to heaven and the physical pain he'd endured no longer mattered. He'd found his peace.

Jesus reminded me, "When you pass through the waters, I will be with you; and when you pass through the rivers, they will not sweep over you. When you walk through the fire, you will not be burned; the flames will not set you ablaze." Isaiah 43:2.

And with that, I found peace as well.

8

That Time My Mother Died

Revelation 14:13

As I write this tea-time memory, the World Series has just ended with a victory for the Atlanta Braves. If you are a sports fan (I am not really), you are aware of the fact that the Atlanta Braves have not won the World Series since 1995, when they beat the Cleveland Indians. They played in the World Series in 1991 and 1992, but they lost. So this is a big deal. The city of Atlanta lost its mind. All my friends I graduated with from high school who still live in Atlanta also lost their minds.

Why do I bring this up while writing about my mother's death? My mother, known to all my friends as Granny Stone, most assuredly the Braves Baseball Team's biggest fan, could be heard dancing, singing, screaming, and jumping up and down in heaven. How I wish she were here to see her beloved Braves take home the 2021 World Series Trophy. Champions! I can hear her exclaiming, "Braves win! Braves win! Braves win!"

However, in 1991 my mother attended the World Series when the Braves played the Minnesota Twins. The company I worked for at the time gave each of their employees two tickets to the series. Since I had no interest in going, I gave them to my mother. Daddy couldn't go because his legs weren't working so well, so my mother invited a fellow teacher friend of Daddy's to go. He, too, was a huge Braves fan. They attended the October 24, 1991 game wherein the Braves beat the Twins to a pulp, to the tune of 14 to 5. My mother, her friend, and the city of Atlanta went insane.

Fast forward to the year 2014. The Atlanta Braves versus The Texas Rangers. My parents indoctrinated my girls into the game of baseball while they were growing up. They became rabid fans. But since we no longer lived in Atlanta, they'd turned their allegiance toward the Rangers. Such a conundrum. We all wanted to see this game. Yes, even me!

By this time, my mother was 98 years old. Although her health wasn't bad for a woman her age, she couldn't make the trip to the game. She insisted, however, that we all go, and she would watch on T.V. She lectured us on not making fools of ourselves and embarrassing her. We promised we would behave.

The night before the game, Mother started feeling poorly. She threw up a couple of times and didn't want to eat. When the day of the game rolled around, she still felt bad. I decided not to go with my family to the game. Mother didn't like it one little bit and kept insisting she'd be okay and that she wanted me to go. I stood my ground and stayed home with her.

By dinner time she felt well enough to go downstairs and eat at the kitchen table. She dined on chicken broth and soda crackers. I didn't want her to overload her stomach. Surprisingly, she ate her bowl of broth along with the crackers and drank a glass of Gatorade. We chatted for a while, then she went back upstairs to watch the game. I checked on her periodically even though I could hear her cheering on the Braves. Clapping when they did well and fussing at them when they did poorly.

The game was still going on when I told her I was calling it a night. She said she felt much better and I should not worry. I made her promise to call me if she should need me. She laughed and said she would, then informed me that my stinkin' Rangers were beating her Braves! I laughed and said I'd come to check on her in about a half hour.

Then she said something that's stayed with me to this day. "No need to check on me. I'm fine. If I die tonight, there's nothing you can do to stop it. It would just be my time." I told her not to say that because we all knew she was going to live to be a hundred and ten. We laughed.

The next morning when she didn't come down for breakfast, I went to her room and found her still in her chair. I called her name, but she didn't answer. When I touched her arm, she was cold, and I knew. I think I knew earlier, when she didn't come down.

I remember thinking, *how I could have slept through this?* Since I'm such a light sleeper, especially when I knew she might need me. But God impressed upon me that He takes care of His children by not allowing them to witness certain things that might give them grief.

As I sat having tea with Jesus in the days that followed, Revelation 14:13 came to mind, "Then I heard a voice from heaven say, 'Write this: Blessed are the dead who die in the Lord from now on.' 'Yes,' says the Spirit, 'they will rest from their labor, for their deeds will follow them.'"

My mother was an independent lady who loved me and nagged me and disciplined me and taught me many things. She could be demanding, but she could also be very kind. She always made sure I never really wanted for anything, even when she said no to things I thought I needed and she felt were not good for me.

The years I spent with my mother are forever a part of who I am today. I miss her still and know I'll see her again. She'll talk about the Braves, of course, and that time my stinkin' Rangers beat them. We'll laugh and I'll say, "Your stinkin' Braves won the World Series in 2021." She'll say, "Yes, I know."

9

That Time I Thought I Was Smarter Than My Kids

1 Timothy 4:12 / Matthew 18:10

WHY WOULD ANY PARENT THINK THEY ARE SMARTER THAN their kids? We aren't, you know. Oh, we may be more experienced. We might even be more knowledgeable in certain areas. But we are *not* smarter when it comes to the ways of the kid kingdom. I know this because when my girls were kids, I thought I knew everything about the kid kingdom. I'd been a kid myself, after all. I hadn't lost my ability to think like a kid. To look at situations from a kid's perspective. Or so I thought.

Kids have the advantage when it comes to being downright crafty in their abilities to spin a situation in their favor. If you understand the word "spin," you know it's code for lying. It's no secret that kids lie to keep from getting in trouble. I've written about this subject many times. If as a parent you believe your kid doesn't lie, then you're living in the land of Oz. They do. Every kid lies. Most kids don't tell vicious lies or lies that cost someone their life, but if you put a kid in a situation whereby he just might end up grounded or punished in some other way, that kid is going to lie.

As parents, the biggest mistake we can make is to think we are smarter than our kids. That we can spot a lie, or even a plot, a mile away. Please don't embarrass yourself by being that delusional. I say this because I have been that delusional.

In my book, *Anyone Seen My Rose-colored Glasses?*, one of the short stories in that book is entitled "Dare to Tell the Truth." It's about my three girls and how they would spin tales so they wouldn't get into trouble. My middle daughter won the lying championship. I soon learned I wasn't smarter than her. When you literally cannot tell if your kid is lying because the lie is so well thought out, I'm sorry, but you're not smarter than your kid. And that was my daughter's gift.

Fear not, because God takes care of parents who aren't smarter than their kids. He provides us with the experience I mentioned before that kids don't have. Although my girls kept me on my toes during their growing-up years, they knew I'd eventually figure out the truth. They also knew that once I did, their lives would never be the same.

Kids can give great parenting advice. Even though they've never had kids of their own, they fully believe in their own abilities.

Once my oldest daughter said, "Mom, don't worry about me doing things I know I shouldn't. I'll eventually grow out of it."

My middle daughter told me, "You know, Mom, me saying my friend's mom lets her do something that I want to do that you don't want me to do isn't a lie all the time. I think the next time I say it you should call my friend's mom."

My youngest daughter told me, "Mom, I think the next time I get in trouble maybe you shouldn't yell so loud. You could hurt your vocal cords."

Kids can say and do some amazing things. It's up to us as adults to guide them through their years of growth by giving them the tools they will need as future adults. When I'm having tea with Jesus, I ask Him to watch over my grandkids. I ask Him to keep them safe and happy and healthy. I ask Him to keep them strong in mind, body, and soul—strong in their faith and convictions. And I thank Him for always taking care of my babies...meaning my daughters, as He has always taken care of them.

Apart from the challenges we might face with our kids, sometimes they truly are smarter than we are. 1 Timothy 4:12 is a reminder of how we must cherish our kids. It reads, "Don't let anyone look down on you because you are young, but set an example for the believers in speech, in conduct, in love, in faith and in purity."

That time I thought I was smarter than my kids never happened just once. There have been many times when I've done or said something only to be called out on it by my kids. But that's okay. Our kids should never feel they can't be honest with us. That's not to say as parents we don't instill in our kids respect for our authority as their parents. *Honoring your father and mother so that you may live long in the land the Lord your God is giving you* part in Exodus is not a suggestion. It means something and is pleasing to God.

God's Word also tells us in Matthew 18:10, "See that you do not despise one of these little ones. For I tell you that their angels in heaven always see the face of my Father in heaven."

The funny, smart, embarrassing things that kids say or do make life that much more interesting. Don't you agree? I recommend that on those days when you feel your kids are smarter than you, don't cry or scream or be embarrassed, simply look at them and say, "You're not the boss of me!" Then go have tea with Jesus.

10

That Time I Almost Fell Off the Chair Lift

Psalm 121:7-8

MY PARENTS AND I DID A LOT OF TRAVELING DURING MY childhood. Being an only child meant I went everywhere with them. Not having multiple kids to keep track of, my parents didn't mind having me along. We spent many summers at the beach, in the mountains of North and South Carolina, and on the Cherokee Indian Reservation. We traveled the Blue Ridge Parkway and visited the Great Smoky Mountains.

My favorite of all the places we visited, after the Cherokee Indian Reservation of course, was Ghost Town Maggie Valley. An amazing theme park with all the adventures any kid could want. I have so many special memories of the times we spent there.

Ghost Town opened in 1961, calling itself "Ghost Town in the Sky." Several years later, they named it "Ghost Town Village." I've always liked its first name best. Sadly, it has closed. Plans were to reopen in the Spring of 2019 but it didn't happen. It's now listed as permanently closed. But one can still hope.

The fascinating thing about Ghost Town was its location. It

sat atop Buck Mountain at an elevation of 4,650 feet. One could
see Ghost Town up on a ridge that extends from the border of
Buck Mountain to the Great Smoky Mountains National Park.
The only way to get to Ghost Town is by, you guessed it, a chair
lift. Or if chair lifts weren't your cup of tea, you could ride the
incline car. We took the chair lift every time.

Ghost Town became a huge hit in Western North Carolina.
I can close my eyes and see it clearly. It had a mining town, a
mountain town, and an Indian village. But the best part was the
Old West town that sat right smack dab in the middle of the
park. That Old West town had not one but two saloons. There
was a jail and a bank. Even a schoolhouse and a church. Other
businesses lined the town's street, but they never interested me.
I loved all the other stuff, except maybe the school.

Every hour on the hour, a gunfight ensued. All the visitors would line up on the boarded sidewalks to watch. I could
hardly contain myself. These guys were amazing. Falling off
buildings, running up and down the street shooting at one another. It was all too cool.

The two saloons, the Silver Dollar and the Red Dog, had
hourly shows. You could listen to country and bluegrass music
throughout the day. I loved it. The Indian Village was pretty cool
too. Visitors learned about Indian life during the Wild West days.
The shows featured a deer hut and a raid on a frontier settle-
ment. Panning for gold and silver could be found in the Mining
Town, and you could see some shows about the mining life. I
remember seeing shows about the Smoky Mountains and how
people lived during the days of the 1800s.

I came away from Ghost Town with exciting stories to tell
my friends. We visited this wonder-filled place almost every year.
One year I had the pleasure of meeting Larry Mathews who
played Ritchie Petrie on *The Dick Van Dyke Show*. What fun we
had together. My parents captured it all on video. If memory

serves me, I was about thirteen or fourteen. Although I missed Dan Blocker's visit in 1963 (Dan Blocker played Hoss Cartwright on Bonanza), meeting Larry Mathews left a sweet memory.

But that time I almost fell off the chair lift also happened in this historical theme park. That summer brought with it incredibility hot temps. Mother, Daddy, and I stood in line waiting to purchase our tickets. Buckets of sweat rolling down our faces made the time crawl by. When we finally got to the chair lift, my legs were hot and clammy. I'd worn my very chic white shorts. I truly thought myself a candidate for the cover of any celebrity magazine.

Chair lifts don't stop. They are a continuous line of chairs revolving around the pully. When your chair, came up you had to jump into it, or it would pass you by. There were ride attendants to help you, so most people felt safe. As my chair came around, I jumped proudly into the seat just as easily as you please. The view going up the mountain was spectacular. I could see all manner of foliage. My parents rode behind me, and I could turn and see them whenever I wanted.

Upon arriving at the top of the mountain and the entrance to Ghost Town, once again the chairs continued to move, so you needed to jump out just like you jumped in. And once again, there were attendants there to assist you. As my chair arrived at the landing, I attempted to jump but my legs had become stuck to the chair! The chair kept going, and I kept trying to get out of the chair. As I passed the attendants, one of the guys grabbed me, pulling me out of the chair and down onto the landing. He shoved me down just before the chair had a chance to hit me in the head. I was a bit shaken up, and my mother, witnessing the entire incident, was screaming at the top of her lungs. It was all Daddy could do to keep her from tackling the poor guy trying to help me. Sounds so dramatic, right? Once I received the all-clear from the management, we proceeded on to the town and a fun-filled day.

As you might guess, tea with Jesus that night before I went to bed was intense. Not on Jesus' part but on mine. The conversation went something like this:

ME: "I could have died!"

JESUS: Remember, my child, Psalm 121:7-8: "The Lord will keep you from all harm—he will watch over your life; the Lord will watch over your coming and going both now and forevermore."

ME: "I guess I forgot that."

JESUS: "Yes, I know. Try to remember it always. And remember I love you. You can talk with me any time you wish."

ME: "I love you too."

JESUS: "Thanks for the tea."

ME: "You're welcome."

11

That Time I Almost Died

Psalm 36:7

THIS MAY OR MAY NOT BE A TRUE STORY. IT'S GOING TO BE up to you to decide at the end. I mention this because some call it a fantasy and some call it a reality. It took place when I lived in South Carolina. I couldn't have been more than eight or nine years old, that age when rumors and stories intrigue the young mind.

My parents and I lived in a neighborhood outside the city limits of Columbia, South Carolina. A fairly large wooded area ran along the edge of our neighborhood. Cutting right through the middle of the woods was a dirt road—a very mysterious dirt road. The parents in our neighborhood warned their kids not to go down that dirt road. My parents included.

None of us kids could understand why this was forbidden, and our parents would never tell us. They said we wouldn't understand. Suffice it to say it just wasn't safe. Now anyone with a brain knows that if you don't give a kid a good reason about why you don't want them to do something, and you make it sound mysterious like an adventure that kid is going to do it.

I decided the only way to get my daddy to tell me about the dirt road would be to get all my friends together and bug him so much that he'd have to tell us. And so, we did. Finally, after days and days and days of getting all over my daddy's nerves, he gave in. He went to the other parents and convinced them that the kids needed to know the story behind that dirt road.

One Saturday afternoon, we all gathered at my house to hear what my daddy had to say.

He began, "Years ago, when all of us parents were kids just about your ages, there lived a family on this very street. Mr. Albert and his wife, Miss Lois, and their son, Bobby Rae. They lived in the house at the end of the street. Bobby Rae's parents warned him not to wander off and to stay away from that dirt road. But Bobby Rae wasn't one for listening to his parents. Curiosity got the better of him, and one day late in the afternoon, Bobby Rae set out down the dirt road.

"Back in my day, families ate supper together every night. The dads would go out on their front porch and whistle for their kids when it was time to come in. We all knew that we'd better stop what we were doing and run lickety-split home. Mr. Albert was no different from the other dads and went outside to whistle for Bobby Rae. But Bobby Rae didn't come. Anyone who knew Bobby Rae knew he would never be late for supper. He loved to eat too much.

"Mr. Albert went from house to house asking if any of us kids had seen Bobby Rae. He said that he hadn't come home for supper, and Miss Lois was frantic. We all knew that Bobby Rae had disobeyed his parents and had taken off down that dirt road, but none of us wanted to rat him out. Finally, Bobby Rae's best friend, Anthony, spilled the beans.

Mr. Albert went home to tell his wife and to get his shotgun and flashlight.

"When he came out of his house, all the dads in the neighborhood were standing in his front yard, shotguns and flashlights in hand. They started down the dirt road calling Bobby Rae's name. At the end of the dirt road stood an old house that looked as though it hadn't been cared for in years. Mr. Albert climbed the stairs to the front porch. The other men came up behind him. When Mr. Albert opened the front door, they couldn't believe their eyes. What they saw horrified them. No one could speak.

"Human bones were lying all over the floor. Some were still together, forming skeletons. Some lay propped up against the wall. There were also shackles attached to the wall and even some still clamped around the skeletal legs and wrist bones. The floors were blood-stained. Each room was worse than the next.

"Mr. Albert told the men to search the woods surrounding the house. They searched and searched for Bobby Rae until the wee hours of the morning. But no Bobby Rae. Days, then weeks passed, and the men still couldn't find Bobby Rae. Mr. Albert and Miss Lois were beside themselves with grief.

"A year passed. One night when Mr. Albert and Miss Lois could stand it no longer, they gathered a few items and set off down the dirt road in search of Bobby Rae. They were never heard from again. Mr. Albert and Miss Lois disappeared into those woods just like Bobby Rae. Some say the ghost of Bobbie Rae pulled them into the darkness of death so they could all be together again.

"After that, none of us kids ever wanted to venture down that dirt road. That's why we tell all of you not to go down that road."

When my daddy finished the story none of us could

speak. In fact, we didn't speak of it in the days to follow. One night when the moon was full and high up in the sky, I decided I wanted to find out for sure if Daddy's story was true or just a scary tale to frighten us so we wouldn't dare go down that dirt road. I crept down the stairs and out the door, flashlight in hand.

As I approached the dirt road, I could hear in my mind my mother asking me if I'd lost my senses. Maybe so, but I had to see if the rumors and my daddy's story were indeed true. The dirt road looked even more ominous in the dark, with my flashlight pointing down. I raised the beam of the flash light. Oddly, it seemed more powerful. I could see a good long way down the road. What was that? I could hardly make it out. I leaned forward and suddenly it became clear.

Three figures stood in the middle of the dirt road. I couldn't move. I stood there, my eyes wide and mouth agape. The figures began moving slowly up the road toward me. I couldn't breathe. Then they stopped. They raised their arms and started motioning to me with their hands. They appeared to be moving in slow motion. I couldn't keep my eyes off them. I seemed to be in a trance. Slowly, they motioned. I lifted my right foot off the ground and started to put it down on the road. But before my foot touched the dirt road……

"Aaah!" I was screaming at the top of my lungs. Something had me by the shoulders. When I turned around, I saw my daddy. He'd saved my life. After that none of the kids, including me, ever attempted to go down that dirt road.

So, let's get down to the lick log. Some think this story is true, and some think this story is total fiction. What side of the fence are you on? If you think it's fiction, then I'm happy to offer you my flashlight and point you in the direction of that dirt road.

Maybe this is just a tall tale meant to be told around a

campfire. Maybe a dream I had as a child. All I know is that after that terrifying incident, I desperately needed to have tea with Jesus. He reminded me of Psalm 36:7 which reads: "How priceless is your unfailing love, O God! People take refuge in the shadow of your wings."

It refreshed my soul reminding me of God's love and my daddy's love for me. And how, no matter what, they would both grab hold of me and bring me back to safety. Jesus also reminded me of the difference between angels and demons. His instructions were to be aware of demons. Never turning toward them or seeking them out, because I would be defiled by them. He wanted me to remember that He is the Lord.

12

That Time I Tried to Dye My Hair

1 Peter 3:3-4

FOR AS LONG AS I CAN REMEMBER I THOUGHT I SHOULD HAVE been born a blonde. Nevermind my heritage is Cherokee and Lumbee Indian. I've always thought girls with blonde hair had the world wrapped around their fingers. Not really. I'm perfectly happy with my dark brown hair. Well, that's not exactly true, either. I'm happy now. But as a teen, not so much.

One of my friends in high school had blonde hair. I loved her hair and wished I had hair like hers. She lived in the same apartment complex as me so we hung out a lot. Weekends during the summer found us always at the pool. The guys flocked around her. I knew it had to be her blonde hair. Guys love blonde hair. Well, it wasn't just her blonde hair. She had a killer body too and that's most likely why they stepped all over themselves to be next to her.

One day I decided to ask her if she would dye my hair blonde like hers. Only her hair didn't come out of a bottle. Her hair came from God. She laughed and said she couldn't imagine me as a blonde. My dark complexion didn't lend itself to blonde locks. But being determined in my quest to become a blonde, I begged my friend to try.

She agreed, and one Saturday afternoon we proceeded to turn my dark hair blonde. I'd spent hours at the store trying to find just the right color blonde I wanted. I had no idea that choice would be so difficult. Ice blonde, strawberry blonde, honey blonde, pearl blonde, champagne blonde, ash blonde, rose gold, platinum blonde, buttery blonde, golden blonde, caramel blonde, and vanilla blonde, just to name a few. I thought maybe strawberry blonde wouldn't be too drastic. Then I thought golden blonde might be better. Finally, I decided on buttery blonde. It just sounded, well, buttery.

With the color chosen, we were ready to begin the process. The steps seemed easy enough. Prep the area, your clothing, and gather the tools needed. That didn't seem very difficult. Always dye your hair in the bathroom. Seemed sensible. Do a strand test to make sure you haven't made a mistake in your color choice and to make sure you're not allergic to the dye. Be sure to apply Vaseline along your hairline to prevent staining it. After all that, you're ready to start dyeing your hair. My excitement began to swell.

Although I wanted to skip almost everything, especially the strand testing, my friend didn't think it wise. After some debate, I finally agreed. She applied the dye to the strand of hair and we waited. And we waited. And we waited. And we waited. What should have only taken about thirty minutes took much longer. In fact, my hair never changed at all.

Totally deflated, I told my friend I couldn't understand why my hair hadn't turned blonde. She said I'd probably need to have my hair completely stripped to change the color. If you're wondering if I did, I'll admit to seriously considering it. My friend, who had more brains than me, highly recommended I not. She told me my hair would probably fall out if I stripped it.

This disappointment required a tea time with Jesus. I needed to know why I'd not been blessed with the loveliness of blonde hair. Why had God not looked into my future and seen the happiness it would have brought me? Not to mention the guy attention. As Jesus and I sat having tea, He reminded me of 1 Peter 3:3-4, "Your beauty should not come from outward adornment, such as elaborate hairstyles and the wearing of gold jewelry or fine clothes. Rather, it should be that of your inner self, the unfading beauty of a gentle and quiet spirit, which is of great worth in God's sight."

My want (not need) to be a blonde ended. I made the wise decision to forego the hair stripping and instead be happy with my dark hair. Oh, the drama of it all. The life and times of a teenaged girl. Many years later, my friend and I would laugh about our many antics, recalling how things seemed so important back then. How every situation was always a crisis. My friend passed away a couple of years ago. I miss her so very much. We shared some fun times together. Especially that time I tried to dye my hair.

13

That Time My First Child Was Born

Proverbs 31:28

AT THE AGE OF NINETEEN, I GAVE BIRTH TO MY FIRST CHILD, a beautiful baby girl with olive skin and jet-black hair. Round eyes so black they looked almost navy blue. Hair so dark and so plentiful. The nurse had so much fun with all that hair. When she brought my baby girl to me, she had curled my baby's hair around her finger. It looked like a little spiral tunnel on top of her head.

When the nurse put my baby in my arms, I immediately unwrapped her like a delicate gift and removed all her clothes. I counted her fingers, toes, checked to make sure both ears were correctly positioned, and I examined her face, taking care that everything that should be there was there. Upon the completion of my examination, I determined that my precious little daughter was nothing less than perfect. I kissed her sweet face and bundled her back up.

Mothers never remember the pain or discomfort they experience during delivery once they look at the angelic face of their child. Now that many years have passed since that day, I can honestly say it hurt like crazy. In fact, I remember the whole day with great clarity. It was in 1972. The night brought with it freezing rain. The labor, well, what can I say? Difficult.

At the age of nineteen, the moment the nurse brought my sweet baby to me I knew I wasn't ready for this. As I looked down at that precious little being, my mind exploded with all sorts of thoughts. My heart rate tripled. This tiny little life excited more joy within me than I'd ever seen or felt in my short-lived life. The days following that first introduction kept me grounded in the knowledge that there was no turning back. I had to learn how to be a mother as we went along. To say there were many days I had tea with Jesus is an understatement. I know without Him I never could have made it.

My little girl, Sandi, never failed to entertain me with the things she said and did. Unfortunately, when Sandi turned three, her biological father and I divorced. We lived in an apartment by ourselves until my parents opened their home to us. As God would have it in His infinite wisdom, He sent a knight in shining armor to rescue us. And when Sandi turned nine, that knight adopted her.

Over the years, it's been my privilege to watch this beautiful child grow into the magnificent woman she is today. Although she's a wonderful wife and mother, she's still my little girl. I still see that sweet little face with olive skin and dark beautiful eyes whenever I look at her. We grew up together, this child of mine and me. Clearly, at the age of nineteen, I had no idea what I was doing. I had no idea what the future held. But God did. Our journey was never easy, but we persevered. God watched over us throughout the years. He stood all around us, making sure we stayed strong through the tough times. And there were many. He never let us down. He blessed us, forgave our short comings, and guided us through each day.

Even today He continues to watch over us with His love and His grace. As parents, don't we marvel at each milestone? I know I do. That time she crawled, took her first step, grew her first tooth, lost her first tooth, experienced her first heartache, had her first date, graduated from high school, went to prom, got her driver's license, and ultimately gave birth to *her* first child.

I've often wondered about Mary, the mother of Jesus, and how she felt as a young mother. I've also wondered at what age she gave birth to Jesus. After researching a bit about the age of Mary and Joseph, I discovered that no one really knows. Theologians initially thought that Joseph might be much older than Mary when he married her. Maybe even elderly. Now they think that it might be possible that Joseph and especially Mary were in their teens when Mary gave birth to Jesus. The consensus is that they might have been between the ages of sixteen and eighteen, given that at the time it was the normal age for Jewish newlyweds. At some level, I felt better about my teenage pregnancy and being a teen mother.

We read in Proverbs 31:28, "Her children arise and call her blessed; her husband also, and he praises her." I love that.

Deuteronomy 6:5-9 also teaches us how to raise our children. "Love the Lord your God with all your heart and with all your soul and with all your strength. These commandments that I give you today are to be on your hearts. Impress them on your children. Talk about them when you sit at home and when you walk along the road, when you lie down and when you get up. Tie them as symbols on your hands and bind them on your foreheads. Write them on the doorframes of your houses and on your gates." Jesus reminded me of this passage in particular during our tea times together.

Sandi became that child who taught me the does and don'ts of parenthood. The one who first called me Mommy.

She is now, and will always be, my joy. My baby girl. I loved her at the moment of conception. I loved her the second I saw her precious little face. I love her now, and I've loved her all the moments in-between.

14

That Time I Graduated from High School

Proverbs 19:20-21

Fifty-two years ago, I graduated from high school. That's as long as a lifetime. Geez. And you know what? I have no idea how that much time passed that quickly. Seems like just the other day I walked across the stage in the Atlanta Civic Center, shook the hand of my principal, and accepted my diploma. Although it didn't happen just the other day, it seems as if it did. It went down like this…May 23, 1970, 6:00 p.m., with a graduating class of 356 students.

In 2020 my high school class prepared for our 50-year reunion. Then the pandemic hit, and we were forced to cancel. We were all crushed. As time passed, things began to reopen, and the reunion was back on. I had plans to attend but, as life happens, I could not. Luckily photos were plentiful for all to enjoy.

For my generation, friends you made in school stayed with you throughout your high school career. I came to my school when I was entering the ninth grade. Before that, I lived in Columbia, South Carolina. Some of the kids in my high school had gone to school together since kindergarten. I felt quite out of place in the beginning. As time passed, I made tons of friends who have stayed with me to this day. In my senior year, I made the Drill Team, which thrilled me tremendously. I loved every second of Drill Team and wouldn't trade that memory for all the money in the world.

I've noticed that my girls don't view high school in the same manner as I did. They enjoyed it, but they don't revere it like I do, and they don't care about reunions. It makes me sad, but then kids change from generation to generation.

You can imagine how we all felt when we were able to reconnect through social media. I can honestly say that's the best part of this type of technology for me. The ability to reconnect with people who you might have lost track of or who you've kept in touch with but are now able to share many more life events.

1970 saw many events. The saddest of which to my group of friends—The Beatles broke up. Some of us sat on pins and needles as Apollo 13 floated around the universe, not knowing what would happen to the astronauts aboard. The U.S.S.R launched the Luna 17 Mission. The U.S. invaded Cambodia, which I'm sure none of us paid any attention to at all. The Chicago Seven went down as 1970 saw an acquittal for conspiracy for the seven but a conviction for inciting a riot for five of the seven. The top movie in theaters during 1970—*Love Story.* The most popular television series for 1970—*Rowan and Martin's Laugh-In.* Good stuff!

As for my high school graduation, I found myself surrounded by my fellow classmates waiting to see who would tell us what to do with the rest of our lives. When they didn't, we all looked at one another with huge question marks on our faces. But there we were, the class of 1970, entering the world wide-eyed and full of…what exactly? The future seemed quite scary. Some of us already knew what we wanted to do with our lives in the future. Some of us had not one clue.

As I looked across the auditorium filled with family and friends of each graduate, I remember thinking, *I'm so lucky. I've got my family, my friends, and years ahead to do whatever I want. Now all I need is a plan.*

What I didn't know then but know now is that God laughs loudest when we tell Him our plans. Proverbs 19:20-21 tells us, "Listen to advice and accept discipline, and at the end you will be counted among the wise. Many are the plans in a person's heart, but it is the Lord's purpose that prevails."

Truly, it was a scary time in my life. My high school graduation brought with it an end to childhood and the beginning of adulthood. The entire world stretched out in front of me. A million choices were available for the picking. Tea with Jesus seemed most appropriate. As we sat and talked about things to come, He reminded me of Ephesians 3:20, "God has more in store for you than you can even imagine." That's all I needed to hear. And the band began to play.

That Time I Went to College

Proverbs 8:11

I F GRADUATING FROM HIGH SCHOOL HAD NOT SCARED THE LIFE out of me, heading off to college did. I attended West Georgia College in the Fall of 1970. When I walked onto the campus with my parents, I'm sure everyone heard my knees knocking together. The campus seemed like a city instead of a school. Even though we'd visited before my enrollment, this seemed different. It seemed final somehow. I'd be living here. Not visiting.

We found my dorm and Daddy, covered from head to toe with my luggage, told me I would do great. No worries. Yeah, right. No worries.

After locating my dorm room, I looked around at the small quarters. On one side of the room sat a small twin bed, and on the other side, another small twin bed. In front of each bed, a desk and chair, with shelves above the desk. Daddy piled all my luggage on top of my bed, stepped back, and wiped his brow.

"Are you sure you brought enough?" he asked with a laugh.

I gave out that nervous giggle pretending maybe I might have left something behind. My roommate hadn't arrived yet. I had no idea what sort of person she might be. I only hoped the two of us would get along.

Mother and Daddy said their good-byes, with Mother hugging me just a little longer than usual. Daddy reminded me of my upbringing and told me to remember he was just a phone call away. As I watched them drive off, I remember feeling a bit abandoned. I guess it's true what they say about only children. We're so used to being around our parents it's hard to let go. And even though my parents got on my last nerve, I loved them and knew they loved me. I knew I'd miss them.

By the time my roommate arrived, I'd gotten my side of the room all put together. Posters on the wall and everything. She dropped her stuff on the floor and plopped down on her bed.

"Hi," I said. "I'm Regina Stone. Nice to meet you."

She looked me up and down and finally said, "Hi there, Regina Stone, I'm Ann Brewster. Guess we're gonna be spending some time together in this joint. Where'd you go to high school?"

I stumbled. "I went to Therrell High School in Atlanta."

"Never heard of it," she said. "I'm from Statesboro, so that's probably why. My parents work at the University there. That's why I picked this school," she said, laughing.

To say that Ann turned out to be the roommate from hell is an understatement. In fact, the words demon seed seems most appropriate. Come the next semester, I knew I'd be requesting another roommate. But Ann didn't return the next semester. I never found out what happened to her. And although she made every situation more difficult, I knew on some level I would miss her.

College went on, as did my classes. It didn't take long for the freshmen to realize that we were nothing in the eyes of upper classmen. We were lower than pond scum. Part of our initial introduction to college was the wearing of the freshman beanie hat. It's one of those many rituals that are very well known and probably the longest practiced—since the early 1920s. Get caught without it on and you wouldn't make it back to your dorm in one piece. To top it off, the color of the beanie would make anyone with any fashion sense puke. Green. Not just any green. Not a pleasing green. A disgusting shade of green. Why green? It indicated inexperience, and we all know a new student is just that—new and inexperienced. I hated that beanie.

Luckily, in the 1970s, there were ways to rid oneself of the beanie. I made it my mission in life to accomplish just that. One of the ways you could do it was to gather a group of freshmen and participate in a rope pull. If you won, you were allowed to take off your beanie. However, this option only took place on the first weekend of the year. You had to compete against the sophomores, and they didn't make it easy. In fact, they rigged the game so you didn't have a chance to win. Eventually, you just became accustomed to wearing the stinkin' thing.

College is that time in your life when your emotions run full circle. Some of my high school friends attended West Georgia, so I didn't feel so alone. We would get together from time to time when we weren't studying, which seemed to take up more time than I ever would have imagined. It became apparent that things had changed. We saw one another differently. Each of us realized we didn't have our parents to rely on. We had only ourselves, and we had to do the work.

Having tea with Jesus became a more frequent event for me. I leaned on Him a little longer. I talked to Him a little longer. He kept me focused and reminded me of Proverbs 8:11, "For wisdom is more precious than rubies, and nothing you desire can compare with her." I needed to cling to that and to know that each day I gained more wisdom, I became more confident and steadfast in my faith.

16

That Time I Got Married for the Second Time

1 Corinthians 13:4-8

HOW DO YOU STEP INTO A SECOND MARRIAGE AFTER THE first one collapsed? It's for sure scary. I didn't know if I should. I mean, I didn't know if it would be okay with God. As I look back at my situation, I realize that God forgives. He forgives us especially when we ask for His forgiveness. As for a second marriage, well, God doesn't stick us inside a holding cell after we make a misstep. He is a forgiving God. We are not blessed because we are good. We are blessed because God is good.

One particular passage in the Bible always bothered me about second marriages because Jesus said it. His words appear in Matthew 19:9 as it reads: "And I say to you, whoever divorces his wife, except for immorality, and marries another woman commits adultery." I couldn't get past that. Then a minister pointed out that Jesus always chose His words carefully. In this passage Jesus never said *is adultery*. He used the word *commits*. He also uses the word *marriage,* meaning that if He didn't consider the new marriage legitimate then He never would have called it a marriage. I realized that although divorce is so bad and *is* sinful, that a second marriage isn't an act of adultery because it is a valid covenant that should still be honored. That the new marriage must be upheld, and the two people must be loyal to one another.

When I met David, I knew he would never desert me. He would stick. And so he has. All these forty-six years, as I write this. We met through a friend who knew, somehow, we would be perfect for one another. She then proceeded to arrange a blind date. A date that took a turn toward silliness. The two of us were indeed silly together.

I'd been divorced for over three years. I had a child. David was also divorced at about the same time, with no children. My daughter was three at the time David came into our lives. We'd spent those three years growing up together. I was only nineteen when I had my daughter, so making it on our own—a child raising a child—definitely had its challenges. Then along came my knight in shining armor. He swooped in and took us into his arms and never let go.

David and I dated for about a year before he asked me to marry him. The night he popped the question we were sitting in my parents' living room. My daughter and I had moved in with them. Trying to pay for an apartment, daycare, gas, clothes, food, and all that's required for life had taken its toll on me. Financially, I couldn't keep up. We'd been living with my parents a little longer than David and I had been dating. So when he asked me to marry him, I gasped. I guess I never thought he would want a ready-made family. But he did. As soon as I caught my breath, I said yes! Six months later, we were standing at the altar of our church saying our "I dos."

Throughout our engagement we faced challenges from family and friends. Those with religious opinions regarding our previous marriages. Me with a child added more comments and speculations. The comments were hurtful. David and I both felt the pain of knowing some would not approve of our marriage. The minister who agreed to marry us insisted on counseling before the date of our wedding. We agreed. Reluctantly at first, but we knew in our hearts it would be of benefit to us both. One of the things we clung to during our pre-marital counseling came in the form of forgiveness. God's forgiveness—not man's. We realized that we needed God's forgiveness to go forward and start over. I'm so glad we did.

When our wedding day arrived, I'll admit I had some big-time jitters. David said he did too. We'd spent the last several months preparing for this event. I wanted something simple, as did David. I did not choose to wear white. I didn't think it appropriate. My mother made my wedding dress. Simple and elegant. Pale blue with cream lace. No veil. A cream-colored hat with the same pale blue material as my dress.

The reason I chose no veil is because of its history. Eons ago, brides were wrapped in cloth from their head down to their toes. This wrapping, or veiling, represented purity. The bride was modest and untouched—a virgin. Since I'd been married once before and had a child, clearly I was no virgin. The veil also presented protection for the bride so that evil spirits hadn't a chance of messing with her happiness. I already knew David and I were destined for happiness. Why then would I wear a veil?

The day came and went with only a minor hiccup. The honeymoon found us falling deeper and deeper in love. I must admit to one mishap on our honeymoon. We were going out to dinner and as I jumped in the car, I didn't see the bee sitting on the seat, and, well, yep, right in the buttocks!

Throughout our married life David and I have had our share of heartache. But the happiness has been more abundant. We've struggled with finances, kids, loss of parents, and flares of tempers, just like most married couples. But we always come back to each other in love and a clear effort of understanding.

When I look back at the days leading up to our wedding, I knew the importance of taking time to have tea with Jesus. My nerves and my emotions were understandably raw. The uncertainty of it all. Me, a new bride (again). David, a new daddy (never). During our tea, Jesus reminded me of Ephesians 5:25: "For husbands, this means love your wives, just as Christ loved the church. He gave up his life for her." and Genesis 2:24: "Therefore a man shall leave his father and his mother and hold fast to his wife, and they shall become one flesh." He also reminded me of Proverbs 31:10-31that fully describes a wife.

In the year 2022, David and I celebrated our forty-sixth wedding anniversary. Our previous marriages are in the past. We've never looked back. We are forever looking forward. Throughout the years, we've been blessed far more than we deserve, and that's a fact. Our children and our grandchildren are our treasures here on this earth and our greatest legacy.

I David, take you Regina to be my lawfully wedded wife, to have and to hold from this day forward, for better or for worse, for richer or for poorer, in sickness and in health, to love and to cherish until death do us part. This is my solemn vow.

I Regina, take you David to be my lawfully wedded husband, to have and to hold from this day forward, for better or for worse, for richer or for poorer, in sickness and in health, to love and to cherish until death do us part. This is my solemn vow.

What God has joined together, let no man put asunder.

Amen

17

That Time I Lost My Cousin

Leviticus 24:17

OUR PHONE RANG AROUND MIDNIGHT ON AUGUST 9, 1978. At the time we lived in Atlanta, Georgia. My cousin Anthony lived in Lumberton, North Carolina. I was twenty-six, married, mother to one child, with another on the way.

Anthony was twenty-two.

I'll never forget that day. The anger. The tears. The asking why. Anthony had gone to a dance held by the Jaycees. The night ended with his body face down on the pavement, with three bullets in his back. The shooter? The guy at the ticket counter.

"Anthony is dead," said the voice on the other end of the phone.

My brain went numb. "What do you mean, Anthony is dead?" I responded, finally recognizing the voice as my Uncle Bennie.

"He's been shot. Shot in the back. He died instantly, according to the paramedics," Uncle Bennie said. "We're all in shock. Will you tell your mother? I don't think I can."

"Yes, of course. And how is Aunt Virginia?" I asked.

"Not good," was the only response.

I didn't know how to form the words in my mouth to tell my mother. It would hit her hard. Aunt Virginia and Mother were close growing up. They came from a family of twelve kids, Aunt Virginia being the youngest. Funny how coming from a large family doesn't mean you'll have a large family. My mother had only me. Aunt Virginia had only Anthony. Just one child, and now none. With the call made, I sat on the side of my bed and sobbed. Anthony and I practically grew up together. I saw him every summer when I visited our grandparents. I loved him.

To say he led a life of peace, honesty, and honor would be a lie. As a teen, he became rebellious and dishonest. He followed those who led him down roads we as parents hope never to see our children travel. Yet, he had a family who loved him. Thousands upon thousands of prayers went up on his behalf throughout his teen years. I grew tired of it watching him do things I knew my Aunt Virginia never taught him. He broke her heart many times over.

My Uncle Willie, on the other hand, never quite set the example fathers should set before their sons. Some might say, "Well, he's not to blame if he had no guidance from his father." I must disagree. He had a godly mother. A family who prayed for him and offered their support at every turn. My cousin made choices.

At some point, we all must take responsibility for our actions regardless of our environment. Too many tears had poured out on my cousin's behalf. Nevertheless, I loved him dearly. My childhood memories of him are precious. However, my disappointment in him ran deep.

With all that said, we never gave up on Anthony, especially my Aunt Virginia. A year before he died, he gave his life to the Lord. He walked away from a life of destruction into a life of salvation, bringing with him a friend or two. Including his father, my Uncle Willie. I celebrated this transformation and praised God for His blessings.

Anthony's life ended tragically at the hand of a man he knew—the guy at the ticket counter. This man shot Anthony in the back three times as my cousin walked away to avoid a confrontation—one that the other man started.

At the news of Anthony's death, I screamed at God in disbelief. How could He have allowed this to happen, especially now, when he clearly was walking in the Word and toward the Lord? After all, Leviticus 24:17 tell us: "Anyone who takes the life of a human being is to be put to death." But the guy at the ticket counter, the guy who murdered my cousin never felt death. Death never came knocking on his door. He never even did jail time. The wheels of justice didn't just turn slowly, they came to a screeching halt. I guess money and power go a long way on this earth.

It was a time of unrest for our family. Especially me. It had a lot to do with the strength of my faith. I hadn't reached that point in my journey where I recognized the power of God's love. I watched my Aunt Virginia's courage in amazement. She grabbed hold of God with both hands and never let go. In return, God blessed her with peace.

Then God sent my Uncle Bennie to rescue me with these words, "It seems unfair that Anthony's life would end now, but God does not make mistakes. He knows our beginnings. He knows our endings. And everything in between. Anthony's life was a rollercoaster, and although he was nearing the top of the ride, God knew this time would be best. Maybe even the only time to call him home. He may not have made it there otherwise."

I clung to those words because in my heart I knew them to be true. As I sat having tea with Jesus, He reminded me of our Father's Word: "Do not take revenge, my dear friends, but leave room for God's wrath, for it is written: "It is mine to avenge; I will repay," says the Lord." Romans 12:19. As I read over those words, I knew I had to leave Anthony's death in God's hands. I needed to remember not to allow anger and disappointment turn into hate.

As my tea with Jesus continued, He also reminded me of 1 John 3:12: "Do not be like Cain, who belonged to the evil one and murdered his brother. And why did he murder him? Because his own actions were evil and his brother's were righteous." The man who shot Anthony became like Cain. He murdered a brother in Christ. I could see that this man's actions were indeed evilly thrust upon my cousin who'd become righteous.

As I write this story, Anthony has been gone forty-four years. Yet I can still see his face and the mischievous twinkle in his eyes as if he were standing right in front of me. I can hear his laugh as he ran across the fields at our uncle's farm. I can even hear him call my name when my parents dropped me off at our grandparents' home for the summer.

So, I celebrate the life of my cousin, Anthony Ray Oxendine, with all its ups and downs. With all its sorrows and joys. I love you, my cousin. I always have. I always will.

That Time I Skipped School

Proverbs 4:1-9

GREENBRIAR MALL IN ATLANTA, GEORGIA OPENED ITS DOORS to the public in 1965, making it Atlanta's third enclosed mall. Like most malls in the 60s, it housed two anchor stores—one on each end with the glorious enclosed concourse in the middle containing all the super cool shops you couldn't help but fall in love with. Anyone who was anyone shopped at those shops. Dress shops like 5-7-9, Casual Corner, and Lerner's were a favorite of my group of young ladies. I especially loved 5-7-9 and found myself there almost every Saturday. They stocked the ever-popular Ladybug and Villager clothing lines.

There were many other shops along the concourse. Jewelry shops, shoe shops, cosmetic shops, fabric shops, ice cream shops, and a couple of restaurants. One restaurant housed a piano bar. Even a drug store and a locksmith shop graced the concourse. You could purchase shoes, jewelry, cosmetics, ice cream, art supplies, fabric, donuts, and a romantic card for your honey. Hats of all kinds, candy, and let's not leave out the guys. Lee's Men and Boy Shop and K & G Men's Store took care of them. Of course, there were the well-known anchor stores that we all frequented. In our minds, Greenbriar Mall truly represented the best of the best.

Hold on to your seatbelts, because now I'm going to tell you about the biggest event that took place at the mall. The year is forever in my mind—1967. My sophomore year. The very first Chick-fil-A moved into Greenbriar. And that marked the time I skipped school. I mean who in their right mind wouldn't skip school for a sampling of the chicken sandwich originally served at the Dwarf House in Hapeville, Georgia the place that launched the Chick-fil-A chicken sandwich?

When the news went out about the new Chick-fil-A, a group of us decided we'd take the risk and go check it out. Oh yes, we did. We skipped school. What harm could it possibly do? Might I just state we were pretty stinkin' lucky that we didn't get suspended. We did, however, get detention. We were spotted by a couple of teachers who also couldn't resist the calling of the first Chick-fil-A to grace a shopping mall.

To understand the ramifications of getting detention, you must understand my parents who, in my mind, were beyond understanding. They certainly didn't understand me. How could I ever be expected to understand them? When they were told of my skipping school (I feel I should write this in a font befitting the sentence, but I'm not sure that type font exists), let's just say I literally saw God's hand come down out of the heavens and slap me into the next millennium. It made an impression, I must admit. Those two weeks of detention gave me a good look into what hell must be like. I never skipped school again.

Some might look at this minor indiscretion and think, it's just kids being kids. My parents, on the other hand, demanded more from me. Skipping school did not appear on their list of kids just being kids. As the only child of two parents in the teaching profession, the very thought that I might even entertain the idea of skipping school, Chick-fil-A or not, caused my parents to lose their minds. And even though time spent in detention seemed like hell, facing my parents was worse.

Lectures. I think at the age of fifteen lectures beat the pants off school detention. Mother and Daddy held the gold medal for lectures. At fifteen, sitting through one of these excruciating times made my head explode. Who does that to their kid? Claude and Evelyn Stone, that's who! Parents don't know what they do to a kid's mind talking about things like responsibility, how it looks to others, what kind of example you are, how it demeans you, putting something over learning. When the lectures finally came to an end, I felt I needed to have tea with Jesus.

I'm not sure what I thought having tea with Jesus would do for my already chewed out behind, but Jesus was having none of this skipping school business, either. Don't think for a second that every time you sit and have tea with Jesus He's going to just love on you and agree that you're a poor pitiful little soul. Jesus loves us too much for that. He reminded me of Proverbs 4:1-9.

Solomon, addressing his son or a student, speaks about getting wisdom at any cost. We read: "Listen, my sons, to a father's instruction; pay attention and gain understanding. I give you sound learning, so do not forsake my teaching. For I too was a son to my father, still tender, and cherished by my mother. Then he taught me, and he said to me, '"Take hold of my words with all your heart; keep my commands, and you will live. Get wisdom, get understanding; do not forget my words or turn away from them. Do not forsake wisdom, and she will protect you; love her, and she will watch over you. The beginning of wisdom is this: Get wisdom. Though it cost all you have, get understanding. Cherish her, and she will exalt you; embrace her, and she will honor you. She will give you a garland to grace your head and present you with a glorious crown."'

Jesus wanted me to understand how important wisdom is in our life. It's the most beneficial thing we can ever acquire. We find honor and safety in wisdom. When we forego wisdom, we can easily fall prey to wrongdoers. Those wicked ones whose goal is to lead us astray. Jesus wanted me to know that when I skipped school, I lost a day to gain wisdom.

After having tea with Jesus, I realized that my parents were right. OMGosh! How could that be? Maybe because they'd lived longer than me. They knew the importance of wisdom. I came away from it all with the realization that I'd traded a day of learning for a Chick-fil-A sandwich.

I must say thanks to all my Therrell High School friends who traveled back into their memories and offered up this list of the stores that graced the concourse of Greenbriar Mall

Binders Art Store, Florsheim Shoes, Oshman's Sporting Goods, Woolworth's, Butler Shoes, Bailey Banks and Biddle, Merle Norman Cosmetics, K & G Men's Store, The Flame Restaurant (the one with the piano bar), Record Bar, Happy Herman's, Baker Shoes, Craft Castle, Zale's, The Magnolia Room, Dipper Dan Ice Cream Shop, Thom McAn Shoe Store, Hancock Fabrics, Baskin-Robbins, Bennet Jewelry, Merry Go Round, Spencer's, Franklin Simons, Art's Donuts, Dotty's Hallmark Store, J.P. Allen, J.R. Riggins, Orange Julius, Franklin Simons, Paris Hats, New York Hair Salon, Piccadilly Restaurant, Lee's Men and Boy Shop, O'Kelly's, The Locksmith, Super X Drugs, Claude S. Bennett Jewelry, Russell Stover's Candy Store.

Who says old people don't remember stuff?
You are so wrong!

19

That Time My Kid Got Her Driver's License

Proverbs 20:11 / James 3:1

WHEN YOUR KID STARTS DRIVING, IT'S THE BEGINNING OF grey hair, white knuckles, and a constant knot in your stomach. When it's your oldest kid—meaning you've never experienced this before—just go ahead and check yourself into a mental institution. It will make life much easier for you.

My daughter, Sandi, turned sixteen on January 12, 1988. This meant she was eligible to obtain a driver's license. She'd spent the previous year in driver's ed learning the basics of driving, which included the written info she'd have to know to pass her driver's test as well as logging several hours behind the wheel driving. During that year, my husband and I showed no signs of distress. We knew her driving instructor accompanied her as she drove the streets of our town. On the instructor's days off, we drove with her. Have I mentioned white knuckles?

Then that dreaded day came. She marched into the kitchen the morning of her sixteenth birthday and announced, "It's my birthday today. My *sixteenth* birthday. You know what that means don't you? I get my driver's license. When can we go?"

She said this in a sing-song type of way. So annoying. Took me back to her three-year-old days.

Odd this child thought she had to remind us of her birthday. Were we not there when she came screaming out of me? Had I not felt every contraction? We nodded and said we'd love to accompany her to take her driver's test.

What a lie! My husband asked if she'd read the driver's manual that would prepare her for the written exam. Did she feel comfortable parallel parking, backing up, weaving through the cones, and understanding that stop signs mean stop? That it's not a suggestion?

She laughed and said, "No problem."

No problem? Two words when spoken by your sixteen-year-old kid that makes you want to throat punch them. We settled on a date to go to the DMV and might I just state I slept not one wink the night before. In her defense, I must admit that she passed both the written and driving parts of the test spectacularly. Don't sigh...the nightmare had just begun.

I'll state right up front, I had many teas with Jesus after Sandi received her driver's license. I envisioned horrible things happening to her on the crazy highways and streets of Atlanta, Georgia. But I never imagined what actually happened.

Now that Sandi had her driver's license, she begged us to help her get her own car. She didn't want to be seen at school driving one of ours. How embarrassing it would be to her for her friends—all of who had their own cars—to see her driving my car or her dad's car. My gosh! They'd think we were poor or something. This is another one of those throat punch moments. Poor? So now we're poor if our kid doesn't own a car?

Well, we weren't poor, but we weren't at the top of the food chain either. Fortunately, my brother-in-law offered us his mother's car, as she could no longer drive. We knew the car was in excellent condition. He made us a great deal, and Sandi now had a very nice car that she paid for out of her savings. She lovingly called it her land yacht.

Over the next several months, things went quite well. No speeding tickets or wrecks. She took excellent care of her car. Overall, we were pleased. Until...

Sandi worked at the hospital as a physical therapist assistant. She loved working in rehab. On the day we shall remember into eternity, Sandi was running late for work. Our other two daughters were home from school and witnessed the entire thing. One would have to know my middle daughter, Noel, to know her thought process. She's my grounded child with more common sense than a room full of adults, even at the age of nine. Her thoughts regarding her sister are that Sandi most definitely has blonde roots. Sorry to all the blondes.

In Sandi's haste to get to work on time, she jumped into her car, turned on the ignition, put the car in reverse, stomped on the gas, and proceeded to back out of the garage taking the side of the garage—bricks and all—with her. It's a good thing the garage door was up—I guess.

A rational person might think to themselves, *Maybe I should stop and get out of the car to see what kind of damage I've done to my car and the garage.* Nope, not my child. She attempted to lower the garage door, thinking it would cover the damage. But the garage door wouldn't go down because she had knocked it off the rails.

Again, a rational person might think to themselves, *Maybe I should call my mom or my dad.* Again, nope, not my child. Realizing just how late for work she was, she kept going. As she cleared the driveway, she took off down the street.

Noel (lovingly called the informer), who witnessed this fiasco, calmly picked up the phone, called me at work, and said, "Mom, thought you might like to know that Sandi just took half the garage off the side of the house. She was late for work." Click.

Tea with Jesus that night took a long time. I lamented over the fact that this might not have happened had *we* taught her to drive instead of the driving instructor, who obviously did a lousy job. But Jesus, in His kind and gentle way, reminded me of James 3:1 which reads, "Not many of you should become teachers, my fellow believers, because you know that we who teach will be judged more strictly." Well, who needs that hanging over their head?

Okay so maybe I shouldn't get too angry. I'm not the world's best driver either. It could happen to anyone. But Jesus reminded me once again, "Even small children are known by their actions, so is their conduct really pure and upright?" Proverbs 20:11.

After having tea with Jesus my vision became much clearer. I should have never had children. Just kidding. I do love my kids—most of the time. We sat down with Sandi and discussed the meaning of responsibility—a discussion every kid hates sitting through. In the end, she understood what she'd done wrong, and the money it took to repair the damage came out of her savings. Of course, she wasn't happy about it, but I offered her a tea time with Jesus to help with the sting. She balked a little, thinking my teas with Jesus were a bit silly. I explained it was either tea with Jesus or sitting at the table with her dad listening to his five-hour talk about the pros and cons of reckless driving. Pen and legal pad in hand. Trust me our kids would rather have gotten a beating than sit with their dad and endure his lectures. She decided to take me up on my offer to have tea with Jesus. She made the right decision.

20

That Time the Man Next Door Tried to Molest Me

Psalm 127:3

GROWING UP AN ONLY CHILD IS ALTOGETHER DIFFERENT THAN growing up with siblings. Sounds about right, wouldn't you agree? Well, of course it does. It's common sense. The one main thing,inherent in all kids who have no siblings is the importance of friends. I cherished my friends. They became my family. Even as a small child, I treated my friends as I wanted them to treat me—with kindness and love.

Some think an only child must be spoiled or have no concept of sharing. My parents never spoiled me, and they taught me the importance of sharing. My mother came from a family of twelve kids. My daddy had no siblings, so he knew my plight. Together they helped me to understand that when you're an only child you have a great responsibility to show your excellence in every way. Now don't get me wrong. I had my moments. Don't we all? But I knew right from wrong. And my moments of temporary insanity were met with a firm hand from my parents.

From birth to middle school, I grew up in Columbia, South Carolina. An Army brat, for sure. My daddy was a drill sergeant. My mother was a school teacher—retired after my birth—but still a school teacher at heart. We moved around a lot but only within the city limits of Columbia. Daddy always wanted the next better house. I was in elementary school when we lived next door to a lady with three kids. She was a divorcee which at the time people sort of looked down on divorce, but not my parents. We liked her a lot. She was a good neighbor and became a good friend.

It didn't take long for me to make friends with her kids. A few months after she moved in next door, her sister moved in with her, along with her three kids. Her sister's husband was in the military and had to go overseas. She didn't want to raise her kids in another country, so they agreed she and the kids would stay in the United States, he'd complete his tour, and return to get them. I loved it. Now I had six friends to play with, which made life even better.

This arrangement worked perfectly for our neighbor. She was a nurse and worked nights. Since her sister didn't work, she took care of the kids, the house, and the cooking. Our neighbor's sister lived with her for eighteen months. Time passed quickly. When the sister's husband returned, they moved away. This left our neighbor with no one to help with the kids and the house. She eventually had to hire a live-in babysitter.

I'm not sure why our neighbor decided to hire a couple. They were young, with a child on the way. At first glance, they seemed like a lovely couple to my parents and others in the neighborhood—especially the young woman. But for some reason, I didn't feel that way about the man. He seemed off somehow. Not that he appeared arrogant. He just seemed different. A kind of person I'd never met before.

As an only child, you're around adults a lot. You get a feel for the ones who love kids, and the ones who don't. The ones who are overbearing, and the ones who are relaxed and easy going. You also have a second sense that detects danger. Radar that goes off, that makes you feel uncomfortable. That's what I got from this guy. I felt uncomfortable around him. Looking back, I know what the air around him gave off. Pure evil.

I didn't go inside our neighbor's house when I knew he was there. I invited my friends outside to play. One rainy day my friends invited me over to have lunch and play some games. My mother encouraged me to go because she knew rainy days were always lonely days for me. So I went. I thought at first that he might not be there. I was wrong.

After lunch, we all gathered in the den to play games. The game we wanted to play couldn't be found. The guy said he knew where it might be and asked me to go with him to get it. I asked one of the other kids to go with us, but he said it only took one. Reluctantly I went. He led me to their bedroom, indicating he'd seen the game on their dresser. As I entered the room, he closed the door. I panicked and reached for the door handle. He took hold of my arm, turned me around to face him, and knelt so we were face to face. I'll never forget his words.

He pointed to my private parts and asked, "What do you call that?"

I didn't answer.

He said, "I know you know what that is. Pull down your panties so I can see it. You know I love you just like the rest of the kids around here."

At that very moment, Jesus took the wheel. I know in my heart of hearts because I raised my hand and slapped him across the face with every bit of might I could muster in my little body. It took him by such surprise that he sat down hard on the floor.

I turned, opened the door, and said, "You better hope I don't tell my daddy."

His face turned hard as he said, "If you do, I'll kill your mother."

He said it with such evil overtones that I knew he would make good on his threat. I began to cry as I ran out of the room and out of the house.

I never told my parents.

Tea with Jesus that night brought with it tears and pain. I couldn't understand why it happened. Had he done the same to my friends? Had he threatened to kill their mother? Were they as frightened as me? How could someone say they love you and then try to do something like that? Jesus reminded me that He never meant for love to be that way. He said, "Love is patient, love is kind. It does not envy, it does not boast, it is not proud. It does not dishonor others, it is not self-seeking, it is not easily angered, it keeps no record of wrongs. Love does not delight in evil but rejoices with the truth. It always protects, always trusts, always hopes, always perseveres." Corinthians 13:4-7.

Jesus made me see that evil exists. He wanted me to know that He would always be there to guide me. He directed me to Psalm 127:3: "Children are a heritage from the Lord, offspring a reward from him."

After having tea with Jesus, I felt better. I knew I had no fault in the situation. Does it haunt me at times? I'd be lying if I said no. It comes back when I hear of kids being sexually abused. I often wonder, during those times, what happened to him. Is he still alive? Did he do it to others? Should I have told Daddy? I know had I told Daddy the guy would have died that day. And for that reason alone, I never spoke of it.

Jesus kept me from something that would leave a scar on my soul for the rest of my life had that man succeeded in his quest. I know without a doubt the hand that slapped that molester wasn't my hand. It was the hand of Jesus Himself.

21

That Time I Helped Harvest the Crops on My Uncle L.J.'s Farm

Ecclesiastes 11:6

MY UNCLE L.J. FARMED HIS LAND YEAR-ROUND, WITH NO days off. He grew corn and tobacco alternately. In North Carolina, where my uncle lived, most of the corn is grown in and around the Coastal Plains, which consists of Fayetteville, Wilmington, and Greenville. My uncle lived in Lumberton which is about 34 miles from Fayetteville, so the soil on his small farm was ideal for growing corn and tobacco.

One season my uncle would grow corn. He'd plant his corn in April—at the earliest, but at least by May so it would be ready for harvesting during the August/September timeframe. I remember it being a sight to behold when I visited anytime from June through August. If the soil is at the right temperature and the moisture is good, you can see sprouts popping up out of the earth about seven to ten days after planting. About one hundred and eighty-five days, the corn is ready to harvest. That's when I'd be there, to help in the harvesting.

Uncle L.J. sold his corn for feed for cattle, hogs, and poultry.

He had no machinery like a grain combine. Before that type of equipment came to be, farmers pulled the corn by hand and stored it either in their barns or corn cellars. My uncle pulled his corn by hand and stored his in his barn.

I remember the mule-pulled crates that slid effortlessly between the rows of corn with the corn pullers (men my uncle hired) pulling the corn off the stalks in such a way it appeared they were dancing. The workers would slice through the husk with their sickle as they twisted, then snapped the ear off its stalk. Then they'd toss the corn into the crate. The mules instinctively knew when to stop and when to start walking again. I watched in amazement at their skill. Sometimes my Uncle L.J. would let me ride one of the mules. And sometimes I'd ride in the crate.

The next year Uncle L.J. would grow tobacco. Since tobacco grew well in his fields, he knew he could get a good price for it. Again, having no machines, my uncle utilized hand labor and his mules to harvest the tobacco. It took a lot of man hours to cultivate one acre. He began in the early part of January, preparing seed beds for planting. In February, he would plant the seed beds he'd prepared. It took even more work to get the seeds to where they needed to be for them to begin maturing. My uncle would mix the minute seeds with some of his soil and spread it over his beds. After that, it had to be staked and a covering (like linen) placed on top to keep the seedlings safe. Then it took about six weeks to sprout.

Tobacco growing ain't for kids. Even after all those preparations, my uncle had to get his main fields ready so he could transplant the seedlings. He used his mules to plow his fields. Then he followed that with disking and fertilizing the soil. After that, the ground was ready for furrows.

Mules were key, and my uncle loved his mules. Their

abilities were essential to getting things done in the field. It amazed me how my uncle considered his mules a part of his family.

The transferring of the seedbeds into the fields begins in early April, weather permitting. When tobacco farming by hand, it's important to know that it takes three people to plant. One person makes the hole in the furrow using a hand peg. Another person places the seedling in the hole. The third person adds water and fertilizer mix to the plant.

On my Uncle L.J.'s farm, you could tell when the tobacco harvesting would begin. When early August rolled around and the tobacco leaves were at their finest, Uncle L.J. and his helpers would hitch up the mules to the tobacco crates and the harvesting would commence. They removed the bottom few leaves first. Every two to three weeks thereafter, they'd go up the plant removing the additional leaves. It typically took three to five pickings.

When the crates were full, the mules would take the tobacco to Uncle L.J.'s curing barn, where I learned how to string tobacco. It's an art form, believe me.

My uncle's curing barn had an attached shelter that went all around the barn. A table-like structure attached to the shelter went around the barn as well. Between the table and the top of the shelter were two small boards with about an inch in between them. The tobacco stringers were all women. They would insert the tobacco stick that had a string tied to the end of it in the slot and take three or four tobacco leaves, stems up, and wrap them around the string so they were able to slide the bound leaves to the end of the stick. They'd go from one side of the stick to the other. I loved watching them. Sometimes the women would get a rhythm going whereby they were all stringing the tobacco at the same time. It was truly amazing.

With the stick full, a runner would take the tobacco into

the curing barn, hand it off to one of the men who would climb the rafters and hang the fresh tobacco. When the barn was full, my uncle lit the furnace. For the next seven days, he'd raise the temperature in the barn very carefully. This must be done to dry out the tobacco and turn it yellow. At this point, it's not a good idea to mess with the dried-out tobacco. My uncle would turn off the furnace and open the doors. This allowed for the humidity of the outdoors to make the tobacco pliable again.

As a final stage Uncle L.J. put the tobacco in what's called an ordering pit, allowing it to absorb more moisture. Now that the tobacco had enough moisture, he'd take his crop to the pack-house. There, he laid out his tobacco. They then graded and bundled it into what they called "hands." Finally, the "hands" were pressed flat and loaded onto a truck, and off it went to a tobacco warehouse. This entire procedure, starting in April, could last until November. That's why my Uncle L.J. only planted tobacco every other year.

One of the things I loved about my Uncle L.J. is that he always prayed before planting, during the season, and right before harvest. God blessed him each year, and he never failed to give God the glory for it.

I loved learning how to string tobacco. I loved riding the mules and riding in the crates. When I had tea with Jesus after a long visit to my Uncle L.J.'s farm, I asked Him why my uncle had to work so hard to produce a crop. It didn't seem fair. But I never heard him complain. I didn't understand that either. I knew I'd be complaining all the time. Jesus first responded, "Because he loves it." Then He reminded me of Ecclesiastes 11:6 which reads, "Sow your seed in the morning, and at evening let your hands not be idle, for you do not know which will succeed, whether this or that, or whether both will do equally well." Jesus told me there are verses in the Bible pertaining to farmers. Genesis 1:11, Deuteronomy 28:8 and 12, Hebrews 6:7, and Genesis 27:28. But Ecclesiastes 11:4 kind of nails it, and speaks to the hard work my Uncle L.J. was always willing to do. It reads, "Whoever watches the wind will not plant; whoever looks at the clouds will not reap."

With our tea completed, I asked Jesus if He would always look after my Uncle L.J., and so He did. Uncle L.J. (Luther James) Bell died on December 7, 1966. I considered him a great man who I knew for only 14 years of my life. In that short time, I saw him as a hard worker, a great father, and a God-loving man. He allowed me the privilege of those summer visits to his farm. He taught me more than I ever wanted to know about raising corn and tobacco. He had big strong calloused hands with a small part of his ring finger missing. He always kissed me on my forehead telling me to be good and to treat my mother (his sister) and daddy well. I loved him very much. I miss him still.

22

That Time I Won My First Book Award

Jeremiah 30:2

I BEGAN WRITING AT THE AGE OF TEN. NOTHING SPECTACULAR OR awe-inspiring. Just day-to-day happenings in my diary. This continued all through my teen years until I had children, and my priorities changed. Writing took a back seat to raising my girls.

When my youngest became a toddler, I decided it might be fun to write a story for all three of my girls. A gift, if you will, for them to enjoy as they got older. One we could read together and then they could read on their own as their reading skills developed. With that, Elizabeth Marie Hutchinson was born.

As an only child myself, I felt Elizabeth's story would play better if she was an only child too, with all the problems and joys only children experience. One thing that's typical for an only child is their appreciation for friends. Having no siblings to play or spar with makes one quite protective of their friends. Elizabeth and I had that in common. I adored my friends and crafted that same kind of adoration for friendship into Elizabeth's character.

With the story complete, I sat with my girls and together

we read *Elizabeth Marie Hutchinson-When I Dream*. A sweet tale of an only child with a vivid imagination. A young girl who, when she dreams, enters a magnificent world filled with magic—or is it magic? She also encounters someone who changes her life forever.

This first story of Elizabeth served its purpose well during my girls' growing up years. When they became too old for this story, I filed it away. Many years later, when my family and I moved from Georgia to Texas, I found the story among some papers in our filing cabinet. As I read it, memories of my daughters as little girls came flooding back. I smiled thinking about the times I shared with my girls reading my story. Then I put it back in the filing cabinet.

A couple of years later, I mentioned to my husband that I might want to see if I could get my story published. He thought it a great idea. And so, I did. After that came another Elizabeth book entitled *Dealing with Margaret*. Then another Elizabeth book entitled *I'm a Detective!*

I'm a Detective! became my first award-winning book. It all began when I met an amazing lady who introduced me to her organization which highlighted Christian authors. She wanted me to enter my book in their literary awards event. I couldn't believe my good fortune and happily accepted. All sounds so lovely, doesn't it? It is. However—there's always that "however" word that can turn joy into something else.

Competitions are good. They can, however, turn ugly. Words like envy, jealousy, bitterness, and discontent can enter into most every competition. Award events are no different. As the event grew closer, I found myself checking out my competition with a judgmental eye. I compared my work to theirs. There were some in my category who were famous already. How would I ever compete with that? Voices in my head taunted me with words of envy and jealousy. I knew I'd never win any of the awards. The competition had become too stiff. So I began to sulk, which on its face causes one to become out of sorts and bad-tempered. I didn't like what this competition seemed to be doing to me. I had never seen myself as this competitive. Or should I say competitively ugly?

The time couldn't have been more perfect to sit and have tea with Jesus. You see, the competition wasn't the culprit. The culprit was me. I allowed these things to enter my mind and my heart. Jesus reminded me of James 3:14-16: "But if you harbor bitter envy and selfish ambition in your hearts, do not boast about it or deny the truth. Such wisdom does not come down from heaven but is earthly, unspiritual, demonic. For where you have envy and selfish ambition, there you find disorder and every evil practice." I knew this to be true.

Jesus asked me if the words I'd written in my children's book were the words He'd spoken to me. I answered yes. Jeremiah 30:2 tells us: "This is what the Lord, the God of Israel says: 'Write in a book all the words I have spoken to you.'" Enough said. My heart and my head became clean. Envy and jealousy had no home there any longer.

With the coming of the awards show, I'll admit I had butterflies in my stomach. I wanted to win, but I no longer coveted the win. The children's category appeared on the screen. When my book appeared, my heart soared. My family cheered. Each book was up for two different awards. One award chosen by a panel of judges, and one award chosen by the readers.

The announcement came for the first award, "And the winner is...*I'm a Detective! Elizabeth Marie Hutchinson-When I Dream* by Regina Stone Matthews. I sat there, stunned, while my daughter kept telling me, "Mom! You won! You won!"

As I walked to the stage to receive my award, my mind went back thirty years, me sitting on the couch with my little girls reading them my very first story of Elizabeth. Never dreaming of something like this. I made my thank yous and returned to my seat still shaking. But it wasn't over.

The announcement came for the second award, "And the winner is...*I'm a Detective! Elizabeth Marie Hutchinson-When I Dream* by Regina Stone Matthews. My mind blown at this point. My family going crazy. By the time I reached the stage, my heart was racing and filled to overflowing with gratitude.

What a night. That time I won my first book award and discovered how vulnerable we can be. How that vulnerability can allow the bad stuff to seep in, turning it into darkness. But when you have tea with Jesus, He has a way of putting it all in perspective. Since that first award, I'm so very happy and grateful to say I've won four more. To God be the glory.

23

That Time I Stole Candy from the Drug Store

Proverbs 10:12

WHY DO KIDS STEAL? WHY DOES ANYONE STEAL, FOR that matter? In my case, the candy in the drug store looked good. I wanted it. I loved chocolate. I had no money. So, I stole it. My stealing came out of impulsivity— not one ounce of thinking about the potential consequences of my actions. I simply took what I wanted.

I couldn't have been more than nine years old. I knew better. My parents made themselves quite clear regarding their thoughts on stealing. In fact, the entire time I stood in that store lusting over the chocolate candy and plotting how to go about getting the candy in my pocket and getting out of the store undetected, I could feel my butt getting hotter. Because should I get caught, I knew my daddy would wear me out. My mother would cry and tell me I was bound for a life of crime and eventual imprisonment. Then they'd make me return the candy and apologize to the store owner for taking it. I'd probably have to learn several Bible verses on the evils of stealing. The store owner might even call the cops. I could indeed go to prison, which would be a total drag as I've never looked good in stripes.

Knowing all this, I made sure I would succeed in my mission of thievery. The chocolate kept calling my name. I loved this chocolate candy. Wrapped in foil and shaped like coins the candies were all gathered in a mesh bag marked *Fort Knox Milk Chocolate*. I couldn't ignore it any longer. The store owner and the clerk were nowhere in sight. I needed to make my move at that very moment. And so I did. As I slipped the candy into my pocket, I looked one more time making sure no one had seen me. With the coast clear, I walked right out of that store with the goods. I'd done it! No one was the wiser. Well, no one except me. And—God.

When I got home, I planned to go straight to my room and devour the delicious treat. As I attempted to bypass my mother in the kitchen, she stopped me and asked where I'd been. She mentioned that she thought I said I'd be over at a friend's house, but when she checked, they'd not seen me. *Oh, dear Lord,* I thought to myself. I'd stolen candy and now I was about to lie. I could see the gates of hell opening, beckoning me toward its fiery pit.

Stuttering a bit, I said, "I decided to go to the playground instead." The chocolate began to melt in my pocket. My mother could usually tell when I was lying, but for some reason this time, she didn't question me further.

I knew if I turned and ran, it would look suspicious, so I purposefully walked at an even pace. Safely inside my room, I closed the door and immediately took the candy out of my pocket. I unwrapped it and shoved it into my mouth. I don't remember chewing it. I think I just swallowed it whole for fear my mother might burst into my room unannounced to question me further.

No sooner had I swallowed the candy when my stomach

began to rumble. I felt sick. Within seconds, nausea set in. I could feel the vomit rushing up my throat. I knew it! The consequences of my actions were beginning to happen. I ran to the bathroom, holding my mouth all the way. I barely made it to the toilet when every stinkin' bit of that candy came rushing out of my mouth. Just when I thought it might be over, dry heaves began to set in.

This is it, I thought to myself. *I'm dying. My punishment for stealing is death. I'm bound for prison. Or worse.* But I didn't die. The dry heaves finally stopped. I reached for a washcloth to wipe my mouth and face. "Thank you, God," I heard myself saying aloud.

At dinner, my stomach still had not completely settled. I couldn't eat much, which caught my mother's attention. She asked, "Why aren't you eating? I thought baked chicken and mashed potatoes were your favorites."

"I'm not very hungry," I answered. "I think I might have played too hard on the playground today." Another lie. My future in heaven no longer existed. First stealing and now lying to my mother, once again. I could see my name written across the doorway of hell.

"Well, eat what you can, then maybe you should go to bed early tonight," my mother said.

I nodded, lest another lie might pop out of my mouth. As I sat in bed, the events of the day rushed back. The store, the chocolate candy, the plot to steal the candy, the awful vomiting. It seemed appropriate at that time to sit and have tea with Jesus. But did I dare? It's bad enough when your parents get mad or disappointed in you, but Jesus? Could I handle His disappointment?

At that moment, I knew I must face Him. It turned out not to be as scary as I thought it might be. Jesus reminded me of Proverbs 10:2 which reads, "Ill-gotten treasures have no lasting value, but righteousness delivers from death." My ill-gotten treasures from that day had not lasted. They'd found their way to my bathroom toilet. I'm pretty sure I heard Jesus laugh at that moment.

Luke 6:31 tells us that we're to treat people the way we want them to treat us. Meaning I wouldn't want someone to come into my room and steal from me. Why then would I steal from the drug store owner?

During my tea with Jesus, He left me with this, "Those who have been stealing must never steal again. Instead, they must work. They must do something useful with their own hands. Then they will have something to give to people in need." Ephesians 4:28.

The next day I went back to the store where my life of thievery had begun. I'd gone into my piggy bank and taken out the money to cover the cost of the chocolate. The store owner spared me the embarrassment of telling my parents. He was truly a kind man. I offered to sweep out and mop his storage room in addition to giving him the money for the chocolate. He took me up on my offer.

With the job completed, the store owner said, "My floor has never shone so brightly." He said I'd paid my debt. We shook hands. I never stole anything again. I learned my lesson.

In the book *The Adventures of Huckleberry Finn* by Mark Twain, he wrote: "Mornings before daylight I slipped into cornfields and borrowed a watermelon, or a mushmelon, or a punkin, or some new corn, or things of that kind. Pap always said it warn't no harm to borrow things if you was meaning to pay them back some time; but the widow said it warn't anything but a soft name for stealing, and no decent body would do it."

I think Jesus would agree with that.

That Time My Kid Fell Off a Mountain

Luke 12:2 and Luke 8:17

MY MIDDLE CHILD, NOEL, ALSO REFERRED TO AS "THE Informer," could not keep from talking if her life depended on it. I'm sure I heard her babbling as she came out of my body. She never met a stranger all during her growing up years and took great pleasure in interrogating anyone and everyone she ever met. The amazing part is that she remembered every detail a person told her about their life.

When dining out or shopping, this child would go up to perfect strangers, introduce herself, and begin her interrogation. I feared one of these unsuspecting souls might decide they'd had enough of this kid and hail the management, or worse, the police.

Looking back on it, I must smile because it's so her. She's now forty-three years old and has grown out of accosting people seeking personal information, but she still never meets a stranger. It's one of the many things I love about her.

Noel entered the third grade at the age of eight and immediately started making new friends along with rejoining other friends from second grade. This year brought with it field trips, and Noel could hardly contain her excitement over the possibilities field trips brought with them.

Noel didn't sleep a wink the night before her first field trip. Neither did I, but for different reasons. When morning finally arrived, I had no issues getting Noel up for school. I found her sitting at the kitchen table when I came downstairs. All dressed and ready for her big adventure. She talked non-stop. This would be the field trip of all field trips. The entire third grade would be climbing a mountain.

My enthusiasm did not elevate to her level. I had my doubts, but the school assured us they'd made the safety of the kids their priority. They weren't climbing Mount Everest, after all. Nevertheless, my mom instincts seemed to be running on high-octane gas. I discovered later this intense feeling I had about this climb had nothing to do with the climb.

"Do you think you can eat some breakfast?" I asked.

"Maybe a little," she replied.

In between bites she sang, "I'm climbing a mountain! I'm climbing a mountain! I can't believe I'm climbing a mountain!"

The remainder of the morning went along as usual, with the addition of Noel's constant singing and grinning. I dropped her off at school with a hug and a kiss and a "have a great time and be careful!"

"Oh, Mom," she yelled back at me as she jumped out of the car, "stop worrying! It's going to be a great field trip." And with that, she disappeared into the school.

As the day went by, I began to relax. No news is good news, as they say. Who even said that? Some idiot, I'm sure. My kid was climbing a mountain today, for crying out loud! Then the phone rang.

"Hello," I said.

"May I speak to Mrs. Matthews?" the unfamiliar voice asked.

"Speaking."

"Mrs. Matthews, this is Jack Bennett with Horse Mountain Hospital. There's been a slight accident involving your daughter, Noel."

"Dear Lord!" I cried out, voice trembling. "Is she okay?"

"She's fine, ma'am, but she did sustain an injury. She has a contusion on her left shoulder. Her school principal, Mrs. Ragsdale, took her to the emergency room where they fixed her right up. Her arm will be in a sling for a couple of weeks but no broken bones at all."

"How did this happen?" I asked, a bit calmer now.

"She fell off the mountain, ma'am."

"She what?" I exclaimed.

"The group was almost at the top of the mountain when she slipped and went tumbling down before anyone could catch her. I'm so sorry this happened, but please know that Noel will heal perfectly. She'll have a good tall tale to share with the other students when she gets back to school. Mrs. Ragsdale will be contacting you soon. If I can be of any further help, please feel free to contact me." And with that, Mr. Jack Bennett gave me his phone number and hung up.

I sat there in total disbelief. How does a kid fall off a mountain? An hour later the phone rang again. This time Mrs. Ragsdale, the school principal, was on the other end. I could feel the need to have tea with Jesus coming on strong. My kid had fallen off a mountain and a total stranger had informed me of this fact.

"Hello."

"Hello, Mrs. Matthews, this is Eleanor Ragsdale with Mount Bethel Elementary."

"Yes, I've been expecting your call. I understand Noel fell off the mountain? How in the world did this happen?" I sounded unbelievably calm.

"Yes, well, it was just one of those freak accidents. It happened so quickly that I don't even know how to explain it. It appears as though Noel either tripped or slipped on something, and before any of us could catch her, she went tumbling down the mountain. I can't even begin to tell you how very sorry I am that this happened. But you'll be happy to know that she has been such a good sport about it. She did marvelously well during the ER visit. All of the doctors and nurses fell in love with her. She does tend to talk a lot, I must say. (Nervous chuckle,) No broken bones, thank goodness. She'll need to stay in the sling for a couple of weeks. I'd advise you to let her pediatrician check her out when she gets home." The woman spoke at warp speed.

"I'm relieved she's okay. Thank you for taking such good care of her. Is she in any pain?"

"She was at first, but they iced her shoulder which helped a lot. The ER doctor said you can give her some children's Motrin or Tylenol if she starts to have any pain," Mrs. Ragsdale explained.

Now that I knew they had everything under control, I asked, "So what about this talking business? I know my child is a talker. Has she said something I should be concerned about?"

And herein my friends lies the rub. Luke 12:2 and Luke 8:17 tells us the same thing. No matter what you do, if you have an informer in your family things are gonna come out. Check it out: Luke 12:2 reads "There is nothing concealed that will not be disclosed, or hidden that will not be made known." Luke 8:17 reads "For there is nothing hidden that will not be disclosed, and nothing concealed that will not be known or brought out into the open."

Mrs. Ragsdale went on to inform me that while they waited in the ER to see a doctor, Noel told her everything she ever needed or wanted to know about our family. My head started spinning. I felt that tea time with Jesus growing ever closer.

I'm sure Mrs. Ragsdale could sense my anxiety through the phone. She said in a most comforting voice, "Don't worry, Mrs. Matthews, Noel's view of her family is something to be envied."

As I whispered a thank you to Jesus, I heard Mrs. Ragsdale say, "Don't worry about all the other stuff. Your secrets are safe with me," and she burst out laughing.

I couldn't help but laugh along with her. She made the situation a lot less stressful. I'm sure throughout the years of being in elementary education she'd heard everything you could imagine.

While having tea with Jesus later that evening, He reminded me of Luke's words and the tragedies that can come from secrets. We all have secrets within our families that we'd rather others not know about. Some of those secrets aren't as important as we might believe. They're mostly just embarrassing. Then some are serious—sinister even. But it's never about what the secret is—it's about trying to hide the secret and the results that will ensue. "There is nothing concealed that will not be disclosed." Total truth.

After Noel returned home and things were back to normal, we chatted about her experience and her conversation with Mrs. Ragsdale. In her Noel kind of way she said, "Don't worry, Mom, I didn't tell any family secrets." We laughed and laughed.

I guess what happens in the ER stays in the ER.

25

That Time I Ran for President

Mark 10:42-45 and 1 Timothy 3:2-3

FEW PEOPLE KNOW ABOUT THAT TIME I RAN FOR PRESIDENT. History books don't mention it. Kids don't learn about it in school. You won't find it written about in newspapers past or present. My family doesn't even know about it. But it happened.

The year I ran doesn't matter, does it? I won't even mention the guy in office at the time, as it's insignificant to my story. Although his inability to lead is legendary. The time had arrived for some new blood. And that new blood belonged to me.

As for my qualifications, I felt I met them all since those who previously held this office weren't as great as they thought they were. But you know how it goes, you got to play the game. One must meet certain requirements if one wants to run for President. The first one is you must be at least thirty-five years old. I've not seen thirty-five in quite some time. Check that one off. Must be a natural-born citizen. Check that one off. I'm the most natural-born citizen ever. Cherokee Indian heritage. Must be a U.S. resident for at least fourteen years. Silly, I've lived here my entire nine hundred plus years of life. That's it? Well, no wonder we've had so many halfwits in the Oval Office.

According to research, older white males are the ones who run and become elected the most. I am not an older white male. Presidents are typically wealthier than most of us. I am not wealthy. Did I want to be President, given this info? Most definitely. I mean, I'm a minority-minority. I'm a female and Cherokee. That put me in a very low percentile. The one thing that leaned in my favor prior to my run was that over the past decade more women and more minorities were running for office and winning. As for President, from 1884 until 2020, twenty-two women have run for President. None of them won, however. But that fact didn't deter me. I'd give the stats for Vice President, but who cares. Not me. I'm running for President. Go big or go home I always say.

Now that I'd thrown my hat into the ring, I needed to get to work planning my campaign. I could hear the road calling my name. There'd be banners with my name on them hung from every building and train depot across the nation.

REGINA MATTHEWS FOR PRESIDENT

I could feel the excitement all around me. Press conferences where I would offer up my vision for the country. My agenda for safer communities. Drain that swamp! Send the violators to jail. Televise the perp walks even. Make our borders safe. Buy new clothes for that chick who only wears those horrible polyester pantsuits. Find out how that guy really invented the Internet. Make sure every old person has someone to walk them across the street whenever they need to get across the street. Create more jobs, and make the lazy people work. No more raising of taxes. Wait, that one backfired on that guy who wanted people to read his lips and follow the thousand points of light. Probably not a good campaign promise for me. Of course, I could always make healthcare promises, but that other guy did that and boy, did he regret it. Backfired in a big way. A candidate should never promise to end a war. That never works, because then you've got to do it. People get emotional about wars. There's always the promise of chickens in every pot and cars in every backyard. No, that didn't work out well for that other guy because soon after that the stock market crashed and plunged us into The Great Depression. Who would ever want that hanging around their neck for the rest of their lives?

I began looking at other promises I could make. Since war is such a touchy subject, I could promise the military not to ever send them to war in foreign countries. No, again not a good promise. Another guy did that and ended up sending every military guy to Japan after they bombed Pearl Harbor. If memory serves me, that guy wasn't the only guy who did that. Another guy sent thousands of military kids to Viet Nam years later. And I knew to stay away from oil and gas topics. Remember that guy who tried to deregulate the oil and gas industry? Things got pretty bad for that guy. Did I dare approach the subjects of what is the definition of a woman, can men have babies, when does life begin, is global warming real, or do we need another gun law? Makes your head spin, right?

So here I stood with my own campaign promises in hand, my funding all lined up, and a never-ending flow of banners and signs. Time to stand in front of the people and make my agenda known. Make my agenda known? What had I been thinking? Why would I ever want to be President in the first place? How does one please all these people? But, alas, I could not turn back. People were counting on me. I could very well be the first minority-minority ever elected as President of the United States.

Time for tea with Jesus. I couldn't take on this huge task without Him. As we sat quietly together, Jesus finally spoke and asked, "Do you know what it means to lead? To be a ruler?"

I stumbled around a few seconds and finally said, "I'm sorry to say I don't. I've always felt these guys just wanted fame and glory and power. Seems they never do what they say they are going to do. Seems like they don't see the American people for who we are. They know nothing about our day-to-day. I'm about as ordinary as you'll ever find. I'm lint on a jacket."

Jesus laughed about the lint on the jacket part, but then He became serious and reminded me of Mark 10:42-45 which reads, "And Jesus called them to him and said to them, 'You know that those who are considered rulers of the Gentiles lord it over them, and their great ones exercise authority over them. But it shall not be so among you. But whoever would be great among you must be your servant, and whoever would be first among you must be slave of all. For even the Son of Man came not to be served but to serve, and to give his life as a ransom for many.'"

That hit me right between the eyes. A servant. That's what's been missing all along. Many former presidents never considered themselves the servant of the people. That's precisely why a lot of them failed. And here I stood getting ready to do the same. Not thinking of myself as a servant. I guess I felt enamored with the thought of being as powerful as the President of the free world. What a responsibility.

Jesus also reminded me of 1 Timothy 3:2-3, "Therefore an overseer must be above reproach, the husband of one wife, sober-minded, self-controlled, respectable, hospitable, able to teach, not a drunkard, not violent but gentle, not quarrelsome, not a lover of money."

Well, it's for dang sure that people who want to be President should take some time to read God's word and reflect on it and even take some stock in themselves. Might make for better Presidents and better people.

Right before tea with Jesus ended, He asked if I still wanted to be President. I stood tall and said, "With all that's in me. I want to be President. I want a chance to serve the people. To make it a better world. To give people hope. To offer them ways to improve their lives. To walk on the side of justice. To give of myself and to give my life if necessary."

Jesus smiled and said, "I already did that."

Yes, He did. But I still wanted to try. So I did it. I ran for President. The experience blew my mind. The crowds were welcoming *and* angry. My voice suffered from so much talking. The towns and states became a blur after a while. I got little to no sleep. My body ached from standing and walking. I heard stories that ripped my guts out. Stories that made me cry for hours. Stories that made me laugh so hard my face hurt. People from all walks of life who simply wanted to be heard.

Each day passed, my campaigning time ended, and voting day arrived. We all gathered around the T.V. watching as the numbers came in and the polls began to close. Had I said everything I needed to say? Had I made my points clear enough? Had I convinced anyone I would be the best President ever in our country's history?

Then I woke up!

Dreams are truly crazy things, and I've had my share of them. I've experienced some scary dreams, some funny dreams, some exceptionally sad dreams, and some embarrassing dreams. In fact, that time I ran for President but woke to find I'd only been dreaming? Now that was a dream!

26

That Time I Bought My First Car

Luke 12:15 and Proverbs 11:14

How scary is it to purchase your first car? If you're me it's pretty dang scary, I can tell you that. I'm not a hoarder by any stretch of the imagination. I tend to throw things out regularly. I can't stand clutter. But when it comes to money—I'm a total hoarder.

The saying, "He'll squeeze a nickel till the buffalo screams," applies to me. I don't know why. I've been this way my entire life. If the price of something is high, I'm gonna debate buying it till it's no longer available. So buying a car for the first time sent me right off to have tea with Jesus.

My parents never bought me a car when I first began driving. Not even when I got my driver's license. They allowed me to drive theirs whenever I wanted. But if I wanted a car of my own, I had to buy it. Which meant I had to work for it. OMGosh! The horror of it all.

When I finally saved up enough money to buy my own car, I was about twenty years old. Now I know some believe my parents should have come through with a car, especially since they had no other children. Twenty years old is a little old to be purchasing a car for the very first time. But my parents were into that whole responsibility thing. Earning your own way thing. Good grief, how did I ever survive? Certainly a tale for another time that I'll entitle *Child Abuse—My Life as an Only Child*.

As I sat having tea with Jesus, I shared all my fears. What kind of car did I want? There had to be a million to choose from even in 1972. I only had a certain amount of money. What could I get for that amount? What about insurance? What type of amenities could I afford? Does the car I want require a lot of repairs? How about annual maintenance costs? If I decide to get a used car—where did it come from originally and why did the owner want to sell it? What about warranties? How concerned should I be about gas mileage? What dealerships are the best? My brain began to hurt. Jesus listened.

Then Jesus reminded me that I should seek the advice of those who not only loved me but would help with my search for a new car. He warned me to be careful not to become caught up in greed and the temptation to go outside of my means. As Luke wrote in Luke 12:15 "Then he said to them, 'Watch out! Be on your guard against all kinds of greed; life does not consist in an abundance of possessions.'" We should never place our wants above our needs.

After having tea with Jesus, I felt better about buying a car. I took my daddy with me for guidance, as well as a friend who knew everything about cars. Jesus had also reminded me of Proverbs 11:14 which reads: "For lack of guidance a nation falls, but victory is won through many advisers." This applies to people as well. Knowing that with my daddy's guidance and the knowledge of my friend, buying a car for the very first time no longer came with all the stress it originally had.

I settled on a Volkswagen Beetle. A good thing because in 1972 the Beetle became the best-selling car in the world, taking the title away from the Ford Model T. How stinkin' cool is that? My Bug lasted a good while. It was a great little car. It remained safe and reliable. The maintenance and repair costs were better than average. The best part of owning my Bug was driving it. I loved it.

Sadly, after eighty-one years of production, the VW Beetle is no more. You can't get a new Bug any longer as they've now been squashed. Too bad.

27

That Time I Blew My Lines in the Church Play

Psalm 37:23-24 and Isaiah 43:18-19

ACTING INTRIGUED ME AS A YOUNG GIRL. I LOVED STORIES, whether they be in books, on T.V., in the movies, or on stage. I wanted to be an actress someday. And it had nothing to do with the glamor or the fame or even the money. It had to do with the acting, the story, and the character. I so admired the talent of the actors of my day.

I tried out for every play at my church or school. Sometimes I made it into the cast, and sometimes I didn't. The times I made it, I practiced for hours learning my lines. Flubbing a line meant complete humiliation, and I couldn't allow that.

One particular year, I tried out for a play about Zacchaeus at my church. We all know this story, right? How about a refresher?

Zacchaeus, the corrupt tax collector came face to face with Jesus one day. He lived in the city of Jericho. No one in the city liked Zacchaeus. They truly hated him. The title of Tax Collector alone made one not so very popular, and Zacchaeus being the Chief Tax Collector couldn't find a friend if he tried.

When the people would come to pay their taxes, Zacchaeus took some of the money for himself. Not just a little, either. He took a lot of money from the people. Everyone knew it, and this fueled their hatred for Zacchaeus.

One day Jesus came to Jericho. The word had gotten out about Jesus and His accomplishments. Everyone wanted to see him. Especially Zacchaeus. But alas, not only was Zacchaeus a thief, he was also short. When he heard the crowd clamoring about Jesus' arrival, he ran to get a glimpse of Jesus. As Zacchaeus approached the crowd, he couldn't see over them. Even when he stood on his tiptoes, he still couldn't see. He spotted a sycamore tree and decided to climb to the top so he could see Jesus.

Jesus spotted Zacchaeus peeking out of the tree. He called up to him to come down and that He wanted to stay at his house. Jesus followed Zacchaeus to his house. This made all the people angry. They couldn't believe Jesus would do such a thing.

After meeting with Jesus, Zacchaeus repented and told Jesus he would give half of what he had to the poor and would pay back the people four times the amount he had stolen from them. Jesus forgave Zacchaeus and told him that God had rescued him. Now that's what I call an amazing tea with Jesus.

I loved this story and couldn't wait to get a part in the play. I wanted desperately to play the part of Jesus. Mainly because my line would be: "Zacchaeus come down out of that tree. I'm coming to your house today." Not exactly as it is in the Bible, but that's how the writer of the play put it down, and I thought it was so cool. Being a girl, I couldn't try out for the part of Jesus or Zacchaeus, even though I fit the height requirement. I had to settle for one of the angry people in the crowd who opposed Jesus inviting Himself to Zacchaeus' house.

Much to my dismay, I only had a couple of lines. The best part—Jesus—went to a kid I didn't much like. It seemed all too

depressing. I felt I needed tea time with Jesus to get all my frus-
trations out. Jesus assured me that I had an important part. The
angry people were essential to the story. Although I felt a little
better, deep down inside I still wanted to play the part of Jesus.

The night of the play I knew I'd be able to say my lines with
no problem. How hard is it to say, "Jesus has gone into the house
of a sinner! Why would He do such a thing?" That was it. Not
very exciting. I hadn't thought about the why behind the story.
The why is that Jesus loves us even after we've done things we
deserve punishment for or even after we're punished. My focus
remained on wanting to play Jesus.

Curtain up! The play began. It seemed all too glorious.
When the part came for Jesus to tell Zacchaeus to come down
from the tree, I couldn't contain myself. I yelled out at the top
of my voice, "Zacchaeus you come down out of that tree right
this very minute!" Ooops. *Not* my line.

The entire church erupted with laughter. I looked at my
mother and heard no laughter coming from her face. Not only
had I blown the line, but the line I'd blown didn't even belong
to me. And I'd managed to disrupt the play. God love the people who work with children. From backstage the director of
the play waved her arms as if to say, "Continue, continue."
And so we did.

Tea with Jesus couldn't come fast enough. I ran up to my
room as soon as I got home. My mother hadn't scolded me on
the way home like I thought she might. The lack of scolding
didn't seem much better. I might have preferred it. Shame and
guilt hung over me like a neon sign.

As I sat on my bed talking with Jesus about my impulsive
behavior and the mess I'd made of the play, Jesus comforted
me. He reminded me that as humans we will make mistakes in
our life. But James 3:2 tells us: "We all stumble in many ways.
Anyone who is never at fault in what they say is perfect, able

to keep their whole body in check." He told me that there's no such thing as a perfect human being. And when we make mistakes, Psalm 37:23-24 assures of this: "The Lord makes firm the steps of the one who delights in him; though he may stumble, he will not fall, for the Lord upholds him with his hand."

Jesus also told me that I must learn to control my impulsiveness as it leads to making mistakes and possibly hurting others. I agreed and promised to work on my behavior—especially my impulsiveness.

It took a while before I stopped being embarrassed about the play. Jesus knew it would, so He left me with Isaiah 43:18: "Forget the former things; do not dwell on the past."

In future plays, I accepted the parts I got and focused on not blowing the lines—my own or anyone else's. I never became an actress. But I did become a storyteller. Which is kinda the same, minus the pay.

28

That Time I Lost My Authentic Indian Headdress

Matthew 6:19-21

WE LOVE OUR STUFF, DON'T WE? I REMEMBER WHEN MY mother moved from Georgia to Texas to live with my family. It took one month of working from 8:00 a.m. till at least midnight every day to go through her house. We had to decide whether to keep, sell, give away, or toss those rarely if ever used items. After thirty-six bags of the toss stuff, we were still left with an entire yard full of things to sell. After the yard sale, we gave the rest to the Salvation Army.

My mother stood amidst it all watching everything she and my daddy had worked for their entire lives walk out of her house and into the hands of strangers. Let's face it, we love our stuff. But now I see it as more than just one's stuff. I see it as the time we invest to obtain our stuff. Tears poured out of my eyes as I watched my mother's face. And now as I write this, I see it won't be too much longer until I experience the same thing.

There are, however, possessions that hold special meaning. Things dear to our hearts. Things we simply won't let go of while we're breathing. I have a few things like that in my life. Good luck getting them away from me.

At the age of ten, I owned one of those things I thought at the time I'd have with me forever. I could pass it down to my kids, and they could pass it down to their kids. I loved it beyond words.

Every summer my family went to the Cherokee Indian Reservation for vacation. I loved looking at the arts and crafts the Cherokee made. (Sidebar: there were no "Made in China" or "Made in Taiwan" stickers on anything we ever purchased. Everything donned "Made in Cherokee, NC" tags and stickers.) One summer my parents bought me an Indian Headdress. I loved it and thought myself the best-dressed half-breed in America. I wore it constantly. My mother had a difficult time getting me to take it off to go to bed.

So another summer, Mother bought an authentic Cherokee Indian Headdress. I couldn't keep my eyes off it. She let me try it on, but it promptly dropped from my head down to my shoulders. I loved it anyway and thought that when I got older, I'd be able to wear it.

A few years later, we moved from Columbia, South Carolina to Atlanta, Georgia. Mother still had the headdress, and I never grew tired of looking at it. Even as a teen. As we began unpacking, the headdress that Mother put in a special box had disappeared. We couldn't find it anywhere. Sadly, we never found the headdress and had no evidence that one of the employees from the moving company might have taken it.

I remember crying over it, and Mother telling me that although we loved the headdress, it represented a possession, and possessions could be replaced. Although I understood her meaning, I needed tea with Jesus. He reminded me of "treasures in Heaven" and what that meant. "Do not store up for yourselves treasures on earth, where moths and vermin destroy, and where thieves break in and steal. But store up for yourselves treasures in heaven, where moths and vermin do not destroy, and where thieves do not break in and steal. For where your treasure is, there your heart will be also." (Matthew 6:19-21) That seemed fine, but I felt my heart needed that headdress.

Jesus continued to explain that the treasure we have on earth includes money and possessions, like the headdress. We can touch our possessions and that makes us happy. Our possessions are a result of our labor. That's why we tend to love them, and sometimes even covet them. But Jesus never said we can't have things like the headdress. He did say, however, "Do not lay up for yourselves treasures on earth." He wanted me to understand that I shouldn't be focusing so hard on the headdress as the be-all and end-all to my existence or my overall happiness.

Treasures in heaven aren't just about tithing, sharing, or being generous. There's more to it than that. It includes living your life for God's glory and the good of others. We see this throughout the Bible. Jesus wanted me to also know that putting the headdress above everything else didn't make good for laying up treasures in heaven. Had I made the headdress a place where my heart was? Seemed so. Jesus understood how this could happen. When possessions and the world become our desire, we're not storing up treasures in heaven, we're storing up our earthly treasures. That made sense to me. I realized that Jesus wanted to be my treasure, not the headdress.

Although we never bought another "authentic" Indian headdress, I've always kept the memory of that one in my heart, and I smile when I look at the photo of my mother wearing it. A true treasure at the time, but not as valuable as Jesus and the times we've sat together having tea.

29

That Time I Held My First Grandchild

Proverbs 17:6 and Psalm 128:5-6

WHILE WE'RE RAISING OUR CHILDREN WE SELDOM THINK beyond next week because we're so busy focusing on the present. It begins with midnight feedings and diapers. As our kids grow, we're still in the moment. Grandkids are the furthest thing from our minds until they are suddenly upon us.

When my girls were born, I couldn't get enough of them. Every second God allowed me to spend with them made my heart sing. God is laughing right now. It's because he knows that is a total lie. Well, maybe not a total lie. A half-lie lie seems more appropriate.

It's a known fact that when our kids are toddlers, we think we're going to lose our minds. Toddlers will do that to you in a millisecond. Then adolescence rears its ugly head, and we know one of us isn't going to make it. It settles down somewhat when they become college kids, or as some say, young adults. There's no "adult" in them; it just sounds nicer to use that phrase. My girls became a little more tolerable during that time.

Then time hits the accelerator and before you know it

wedding bells are going off everywhere. You cry because you'll miss them and, if truth be told, your control. My husband and I are blessed that our girls chose very good men. But then time hits the accelerator again and the next thing you know you're a grandma or memaw or nana or Mawmaw or granny or whatever the little creature wants to call you.

When my daughter announced her pregnancy with her first child (our first grandchild), I couldn't control my excitement. A baby! A precious baby who would grow up to call me grandma. My daughter served in the military at the time, stationed in England. I felt helpless. I couldn't be with her through each of her stages of pregnancy, which made me very sad indeed. The cost to go overseas was out of my reach. So we sent letters and called to keep in touch. I had tea with Jesus several times during my daughter's pregnancy, asking Him not only for her good health and the health of the baby but for patience on my part. He laughed at the patience request, as He knows me.

Then it happened. On April 12th in the year of our Lord 1994, our first grandchild arrived. A precious little girl. Danielle Elizabeth woke the world up with her presence. She chose this day, I suspect, because she somehow knew it was also her great-grandparents' wedding anniversary and wanted to be part of that celebration as well. With red hair blazing, this kid spectacularly burst into our lives. It would be six months after Danielle's birth before we could meet her. When that day arrived and we could finally hold her and smooch all over her face, we had no way of knowing how much joy she would bring to our lives.

As I held my first grandchild in my arms, every emotion known to man washed over me. I became that frightened nineteen-year-old girl holding her baby for the first time. Just like her mother, this precious bundle of love and joy had my blood flowing through her veins. Seemed like being a grandma for the first time resembled being a mother for the first time in many ways.

Tea with Jesus held a different feel after holding Danielle. I had so many questions regarding my role. I'd never been a grandma before. Do I spoil her rotten or what? Jesus laughed, because He knows me. Of course, I'd spoil her rotten. But within boundaries, Jesus reminded me. He also reminded me of Proverbs 17:6, which reads: "Children's children are a crown to the aged, and parents are the pride of their children." Seemed simple enough. But is it really that simple?

Over the years I've watched this precious creature as she's developed into a magnificent woman. As we enter into chapter twenty-eight of the book of Danielle, I can't help but state that I love this kid beyond measure. Beyond that, I like her so very much. I wouldn't trade one second I've had the pleasure of spending with her. My one regret is that I don't get to see her enough. I will forever be in her corner. I am her biggest fan.

As I write this, we have just returned home from attending Danielle's wedding. A couple of years ago she met a young man who God sent to be her knight in shining armor. They are now Mr. and Mrs. Chris Larkin. My mother always called Danielle Princey since she was born in England. I guess Mother always believed that a knight would come along and become Danielle's prince. And that's exactly what happened.

When we returned from Danielle's wedding, full of joy and peace, I felt the need to sit and have tea with Jesus. I wanted to know how we got here so quickly. How it seemed like yesterday when I first held Danielle in my arms. Jesus smiled and said, "I'm sure it does. But the wonderful thing about time is that it offers with it an opportunity to gather knowledge. As a grandma, you'll be able to offer your granddaughter the knowledge her mother can't. You're still teaching your daughter things. That's the joy of being a grandma."

Jesus left me with this from Psalm 128:5-6: "May the Lord bless you from Zion; may you see the prosperity of Jerusalem all the days of your life. May you live to see your children's children—peace be on Israel."

Tea with Jesus always helps. Since that first time I held Danielle, I've held five more grandchildren. Skye and Dylan who call me Memaw. Haylie and Finley who call me Mawmaw. It will be interesting to see what Noah calls me. I wonder when Danielle and Chris decide to have kids what it will be like to be a great-grandma! OMGosh!

30

That Time I Watched My Daughter Graduate from College

Proverbs 4:13 and Proverbs 23:24-25

AS PARENTS, WE HAVE THESE "CUP OVERFLOWING" MOMENTS with our kids. The times when they shine brighter than normal. Let's face it, kids are tough acts. They try your patience. They take up all your time. They crack your heart. But you love them and want the best for them, so you put forth the effort.

My kids have done some spectacular things throughout their lives. They've also done some pretty stupid things. As have I. The best part when looking back over all those times is that they represent the dash. You know that poem about the dash? How we spend our time—that dash between birth and death. Thankfully, my girls are still in that dash part. But from time to time I look back and remember both—the spectacular and the stupid.

Having tea with Jesus during all those times has brought me closer to His word and my faith. That's not to say I don't have those moments of craziness when I throw my hands in the air and rant, "What's the point?" Loudly. Jesus has that way of helping me see that in good and trying times, He's always available to have tea with me.

My youngest daughter, Ashlee, wanted to be a doctor. She talked about it all the time. When she graduated from high school, she told us she'd decided to go into pediatrics. We knew how much she loved kids and encouraged her in her decision.

Ashlee is that kid who is an over-achiever. She's been that way her entire life. Perfection should have been her middle name. She overthinks everything. Her beginning in this world was rough. The delivery seemed to last an eternity. There were complications. We didn't know if she would make it. But God was in that OR with us the entire time, and this kid showed her warrior princess side to us all. With the umbilocal cord wrapped around her neck, the oxygen to her brain was cut off. She came out of me as blue as a Smurf. It would be a couple of days before I could see her.

She overcame many challenges in her life, including several years of speech therapy, hours of studying, and more hours of practicing her words and vocabulary. When she began school, I found myself constantly telling her it was time to stop studying. Over the years I've watched that same determination grow right along with her. A true perfectionist, a hard worker, a great friend, a total crier, and a bit of a mama's girl, Ashlee is truly one of a kind. When I look at her now, I see that little face that used to look up at me with tears in her eyes, determined to soar past her difficulties. Determined to learn all she could. Determined to grab hold of life and shake it for all its worth.

I knew she would be a great doctor. True to her nature, she took on way too many subjects in her first semester of college. I told her, "Ashlee, you can't graduate from college in your first semester." She ignored me.

Reality set in when she received a "D" in biology. She went

nuts and wrote a scathing email to her professor. A "D" had never appeared on any paper or report card in her entire educational career. At that point she decided if she couldn't do better in biology how would she then become a doctor?

She came to us and said, "I'm not going to be a doctor. A "D" is unacceptable. I'm going to get my degree in elementary education and become a teacher."

I had to stifle my laugh. Don't judge. I had to. This was typical Ashlee. I said to her, "That's fine, kiddo. Whatever you want to do we'll support you in every way we can. Just understand that a doctor's salary is up here. Teacher salary down here." I motioned this with my hands. She laughed and said she got it.

After all of this, I decided tea with Jesus seemed most appropriate. I needed to know that I'd directed her correctly. Had I conveyed to her the importance of making the right decision? Jesus assured me I had. He reminded me of the value of education as written in Proverbs 4:13 which reads: "Hold on to instruction, do not let it go; guard it well, for it is your life."

When Ashlee graduated from college, we couldn't have been more proud. Everything she'd accomplished in spite of her struggles. God watched over her the entire time. As I watched my daughter accept her diploma, I thought, *Look at you, sweet girl. You did it. All the hard work was worth it.*

During tea with Jesus, I wanted to know if being so proud of my daughter conflicted with anything His word teaches us. Pride is never good. It leads to all manner of evil. I've always made it a point to encourage my children in their endeavors. They know how much I admire them. But I also wanted them to know where their abilities come from. Our abilities and our accomplishments come from God's grace. My prayers for my children and grandchildren always contain gratitude to God for His grace. I've wanted my girls to know that all they do should be done for the glory of God.

Jesus helped me to understand that it's perfectly okay to be proud of your kids. Proverbs 23:24-25 speaks to this fact: "The father of a righteous child has great joy; a man who fathers a wise son rejoices in him. May your father and mother rejoice; may she who gave you birth be joyful!" That's what I felt—joy—as I watched Ashlee on stage accepting her college diploma.

Benjamin Franklin is quoted as saying several things about this.

"The Bible is the foundation of all education and development."

"The greatest education is the knowledge of God."

"An investment in knowledge pays the best interest."

Thanks, Ben!

Now, all these years later, as God would have it, Ashlee is a magnificently gifted teacher. Her students adore her. It's been my honor to witness the birth, growth, maturity of mind, and development of character of this wonderful creature. Not to mention she's an amazing mother.

31

That Time I Saw the Wreckage of the Twin Towers in NYC

Revelation 22:10-12 and Proverbs 6:12-15

EVERYONE REMEMBERS WHERE THEY WERE AND WHAT THEY were doing on the morning of September 11, 2001. When 9/11 falls on a Sunday, I'm always grateful to be sitting in God's house. On this one particular Sunday—September 11, 2017—I decided to look back over some of my writings about that day. I came upon something I wrote on Sunday, September 11, 2016. It reads: In Church today we talked about 9/11 and living each day with courage. It's wonderful to know that no matter the circumstance, no matter the event, and no matter the emotion, God's Word speaks directly to it.

As we remember those lost on that day when the world stopped turning, when the earth took on an eerie silence, and when we watched the tragedy unfold before our eyes, Psalm 27:1-5, 13-14 offers us a path to find our way to courage and away from fear:

"The Lord is my light and my salvation—whom shall I fear? The Lord is the stronghold of my life—of whom shall I be

118

afraid? When the wicked advance against me to devour me, it is my enemies and my foes who will stumble and fall. Though an army besiege me, my heart will not fear; though war break out against me, even then I will be confident. One thing I ask from the Lord, this only do I seek: that I may dwell in the house of the Lord all the days of my life, to gaze on the beauty of the Lord and to seek him in his temple. For in the day of trouble he will keep me safe in his dwelling; he will hide me in the shelter of his sacred tent and set me high upon a rock. I remain confident of this: I will see the goodness of the Lord in the land of the living. Wait for the Lord; be strong and take heart and wait for the Lord." Great words.

However, as I sat in my living room on that very day September 11, 2001, I wasn't thinking of Psalm 27. My heart breaking into a million pieces, I felt as if I were in a dreamscape and not reality. I remember thinking how would we ever go on? Psalm 27 tells us we will always go on in the Lord. We will never be alone. And, yes, we must be strong and take heart. But those words stood at bay outside my mind that morning. My anger grew with every word I heard on T.V. With every scene.

I still weep when I hear the sounds and see the sights of that awful day. The screams, the crashing down of buildings, the senseless loss of life, the people in the streets running for their lives, the total devastation of it all. For what? Hate. I'll never understand it.

I remember the urgency to sit and have tea with Jesus after spending an entire day watching the coverage of this horrific tragedy. He comforted me and allowed me to rant and cry. Then He reminded me of our Father's power and strength. We read in Proverbs 6:12-15: "A troublemaker and a villain, who goes about with a corrupt mouth, who winks maliciously with his eye, signals with his feet and motions with his fingers, who plots evil with deceit in his heart—he always stirs up conflict. Therefore disaster will overtake him in an instant; he will suddenly be destroyed—without remedy." Those words helped.

Jesus also reminded me of Revelation 22:10-12: "Then he told me, 'Do not seal up the words of the prophecy of this scroll, because the time is near. Let the one who does wrong continue to do wrong; let the vile person continue to be vile; let the one who does right continue to do right; and let the holy person continue to be holy. Look, I am coming soon! My reward is with me, and I will give to each person according to what they have done.'" That set well with me.

A couple of years after 9/11, I visited New York City. I went to Ground Zero. The city had constructed a fence around the area where the Twin Towers once stood. Cranes and bulldozers were digging and moving debris around. The sight of such horror struck me to my core. I wept. All the visions of that day came rushing back. I stood there for I don't know how long taking it all in. Remembering. I'd visited New York City a few years before 2001. I'd walked through the Twin Towers and marveled at their structure. Now look at what was left.

I needed to sit with Jesus. He comforted me once more as He'd done the day of September 11th. He wanted me to know that there will always be evil things that will happen in this world until He returns. I felt relieved that He never asked me to forget. He did remind me of Proverbs 6:16-19 which reads: "There are six things the Lord hates, seven that are detestable to him: haughty eyes, a lying tongue, hands that shed innocent blood, a heart that devises wicked schemes, feet that are quick to rush into evil, a false witness who pours out lies and a person who stirs up conflict in the community."

I replied, "Yes, thank you, Jesus."

The memories of 9/11 and the days that followed are forever etched in my mind. I will never forget. I never see a picture or a video of that day that I don't cry and mourn the lives lost.

I will never forget. In those days that followed as I felt that air of silence over our land, I know it will continue to haunt me forever. I will never forget.

On September 11, 2001, by dawn's early light, evil crept in and stole our innocence and the lives of our citizens. I will *never* forget.

32

That Time I Got Baptized

Acts 2:38

I REMEMBER MY BAPTISM LIKE IT HAPPENED YESTERDAY. AT THE AGE of nine, I decided to give my life to Christ. I told my parents I wanted to be baptized. I knew in my heart I wanted this more than anything. Yes, even at age nine. Now I'm not sure if I understood the term renewal, but I knew I loved Jesus, and I wanted Him to know just how much I loved Him by being baptized. That's not to say there haven't been times when I felt the need to rededicate my life. Those were the times when I found my life spinning out of control. Times when I knew the path I'd chosen was the wrong one. But the day of my baptism is a memory I cherish. My parents made it such a special day, and I'll always be grateful for that.

We were Baptist. We didn't do the sprinkling thing or the infant dabbing a little water on the head thing and call it a baptism. Nope, Baptists believe in total submersion. Admittedly, I was nervous about this procedure. Our minister was a little elderly in my mind, so the thought of slipping out of his arms or not being able to fully hold my nose was a concern. I've always had a fear of drowning, which made the prospect of some old guy holding me under the water a bit daunting. Obviously, I didn't drown, and the old chap did a great job of making me feel safe. And although I looked like a drowned rat afterward, I felt renewed. Even if I didn't know what that meant.

I remember the day before my baptism, I needed to have tea with Jesus in a big way. I needed to make sure I'd made the right decision. Did I understand the true meaning? Jesus explained to me the importance of baptism and brought forth to me Acts 2:38 as it reads: "Peter replied, 'Repent and be baptized, every one of you, in the name of Jesus Christ for the forgiveness of your sins. And you will receive the gift of the Holy Spirit.'" He pointed out the words "every one of you." I knew that included me.

Many remember the story of Jesus being baptized by John the Baptist, or John the Baptizer, as my Methodist minister friend called him. It's found in the gospels of Matthew, Mark, and Luke. Can you imagine being a part of the crowd that stood around and watched what some theologians view as a historical event? I view it as simply heart-warming and humbling and not necessarily an event. Certainly humbling for John, who felt Jesus should be the one baptizing him. I get that completely.

Jesus instructed his disciples to go out into the world and baptize. I believe that's why Jesus thought it important that He should be baptized. He wanted to show others the importance of being renewed. Baptism can bring such a wonderful renewal to our lives. It gives us an identity. Jesus was God's beloved son. It was His identity. But Jesus also knew He must receive baptism because He needed to be the example. God claims us in baptism. Without it, we can be insecure and this insecurity can cause us to make mistakes.

Baptism assures us that God has forgiven our sins. I submit there are those among us who don't know they need forgiveness. But the Bible is clear about all of us needing forgiveness.

The Bible tells us that all can be forgiven. If we confess our sins, God will forgive us. And with that forgiveness, we discover a renewal that changes our lives. In Baptism God gives each of us purpose, which ultimately is God's purpose for our lives.

My baptism day is a day I'll always remember. And not because I got a truckload of gifts either. Or even that my mother made me all of my favorite foods. I remember it because my parents made it a point to explain the importance of renewal through baptism. Although come to think of it, that charm bracelet I got was kinda cool. Ultimately, having tea with Jesus helped the most.

I don't have pictures of my baptism, but I do of my grandkids' baptisms, Skye, Haylie, Finley, and Noah. And my son-in-law, Jeremie. Skye wasn't baptized in the same manner as the others. Skye is Baptist. The rest of the gang is Methodist. You can see the different styles of baptism in the Baptist church and the Methodist church. Skye, being Baptist, got immersed. Haylie, Finley, Noah, and Jeremie got sprinkled.

Now I know there are millions of articles that speak to the differences in baptism between the Baptist and the Methodist church. They understand baptism differently. However, they both agree baptisms should occur publicly and that the church should hold the baptized person accountable for the Christian life they've been baptized into.

In my mind, regardless of the how, it took. And that's all that matters to me.

That Time My Husband Retired

Ephesians 4:2-3

MY HUSBAND RETIRED AFTER WORKING FROM HIS TEENAGE years until the age of sixty-eight. He worked hard to provide for himself and then his family. Looking back, he said he had no regrets. Some jobs were a struggle, but he always did his best. His final job lasted well over twenty years. He loved it. He traveled a lot, something he enjoyed. He loved being in the medical field, but retirement was upon him.

I'm convinced that when our husbands retire no one thinks of the wife and how it affects her. Especially wives who are home or who work from home. It doesn't much affect those who are still in the workplace until they come home from work and find their husband has all but destroyed the house. I was the wife who worked from home. Not only did I work from home, but I also cared for our granddaughter. My plate overflowed.

As a total OCD individual, I hold to a strict schedule. My days flowed perfectly until my husband retired. He disrupted everything. In the beginning, he awoke at 6:00 a.m. and began roaming around the house getting into things. Finally, he decided to start working on all the things he never had time to work on when he had a job. He built a cooler, cleaned out his shed, weeded and reworked the flower beds, and cleaned out the garage.

With all that accomplished, he began invading my space once more, thinking it a good idea to rearrange my pantry. If there's one thing an OCD person hates, it's someone messing with their space. We finally had to have a come to Jesus meeting. It didn't take.

My husband decided I needed help with our granddaughter, Haylie. Let it be known that it is not easy to get babies on a schedule. Luckily Haylie had inherited some of my OCD tendencies and adapted well to the baby schedule. My husband, in all his eagerness to help, made a mess of things. Haylie let him know in no uncertain terms that she liked her schedule and had no use for his interruptions.

With our schedules disrupted and my pantry in disarray, I contacted several friends and begged them to invite my husband to lunch, to play golf, to go do guy stuff—anything to get him out of my hair. These people were of no help whatsoever. I'd hoped he'd be gone for at least a year, but they only took him away for a couple of days. Losers. Time for tea with Jesus.

With my nerves frayed and my OCD in overdrive, I met Jesus for tea, knowing He would be the one to help. I love my husband and try not to hurt his feelings. But I knew I was getting ready to do just that if I hadn't already done it. Jesus said the one word that He knew I'd react to—patience. Not my best quality. Jesus knew this, so He hit me with it knowing it would get my attention. He reminded me of Ephesians 4:2-3 as it reads: "Be completely humble and gentle; be patient, bearing with one another in love. Make every effort to keep the unity of the Spirit through the bond of peace." I hadn't done that.

Jesus explained that retirement, although welcomed by most since they've spent their lives working toward it, is unsettling at first. People simply don't know what to do with themselves. They're used to a schedule. Getting up, getting dressed, eating breakfast, hopping in the car, and fighting the traffic to work. Busyness fulfills our need for usefulness. And if we love our job as my husband did, retirement can also be a loss.

Psalm 71:18 explains that thought even better as it reads: "Even when I am old and gray, do not forsake me, my God, till I declare your power to the next generation, your mighty acts to all who are to come." Jesus explained that with my patience (nudge) and time, my husband would settle into his retirement and would no longer be a pain but a helper.

Now years into my husband's retirement, he has become just that—a helper. We work better together. Like Ecclesiastes 4:9 reads: "Two are better than one, because they have a good return for their labor." He's sleeping in and not getting up so early. We're on a schedule because now we take care of two grandkids. I'm semi-retired yet still busy, which is therapeutic for us OCD crazies. But the best part is that he ain't messing up my pantry!

34

That Time I Said Goodbye to Horace and Charles

2 Corinthians 5:7/Isaiah 41:10/Hebrews 13:7/ Jeremiah 3:15/Proverbs 27:9

M Y PAPA ALWAYS TOLD ME THAT THERE ARE THOSE WHO God calls to minister. Not preach—minister. We get those two words confused. I'd much rather listen to a minister than a preacher. A preacher is defined as a person who delivers a sermon publicly. That's it? That's all you got? On the other hand, a minister is defined as a member of the clergy, especially in Protestant churches. Ugh. We must look beyond that definition because a minister when defined as a verb is: *attends to the needs of.* That's what I've always looked for in a church. Does this particular church have a minister or a preacher?

Horace B. Youngblood and Charles A. Sineath represent two men in my life who I will never forget and will forever love. Yes, my husband knows about them. Horace came into my life when I was a child. Charles came into my life when I was a young mother.

Let's begin with Horace Youngblood. Boy oh, boy did my family love this guy. He and his wife, Bennie, as everyone called her, were not only the leaders of our church but dear friends. I discovered her obituary as I began my research for this story and read that she passed away on June 7, 2012. Not so very long ago. I searched and searched for Horace's obituary to no avail. I did, however, discover that he passed away in March of 2005.

My family's church, Woodfield Park Baptist Church, held its first worship service on June 19, 1960. It began as a small congregation with about eighty-three people meeting in a seven-room home close to Fort Jackson Military base where I was born in 1952. We didn't attend the church at the time of its first worship service so I can't speak to its members or its minister.

Then in 1961 along came Rev. Horace B. Youngblood. Horace became Woodfield Park's first full-time minister. His first service took place on Easter Sunday, April 2, 1961. And that's the day my family and I began attending. Under his leadership, the church grew like crazy and soon needed additional space. Horace had many talents and made arrangements to purchase a surplus Army chapel from Fort Jackson. The leaders of the church decided to move the structure (church) from the base onto some property they owned. They then renovated and extended the church. On June 13, 1965, the good people of Woodfield Park Baptist Church held their first worship service in their new church, led by Horace. The cool part about it all is that this very structure is still in use to this day and seats about four hundred people.

Horace Youngblood set the path for me that led to Christianity. He had a hand in shaping who I would become as a Christian. When we began attending Woodfield Park in 1961, I was nine years old. As the church grew, so did I. Horace and his sweet wife, Bennie, visited with us at our home on many occasions. My parents believed in making sure they knew their minister at every level. I can see with great clarity all the times we spent together.

Horace had a way of captivating his congregation with his sermons. Even at the age of nine, I understood most of them. You learn in presenting (regardless of the topic) that complexity is boring, leads to disconnect, and is difficult to follow. Horace kept it simple. He used the KISS method. So regardless of your age, as you sat and took in his message—you got it. He was that good. I loved him.

One of my sweetest memories of Horace was how he conducted the Lord's Supper. He always held it at night. Sunday, of course, but always at night. After the elements were taken, Horace would say a few words and then dismiss us. He requested we not speak. No visiting while inside the church, and no visiting out in the parking lot. We simply gathered our belongings and exited the church in total silence. One might think this odd or even a little much for a kid to experience, but it made an impression on me. It taught me the true meaning of respect.

In 1966 we moved from Columbia, South Carolina to Atlanta, Georgia due to a job opportunity for my daddy. He accepted a teaching job that he considered too good to pass up. I needed tea with Jesus desperately. As we sat together the first two Bible verses Jesus reminded me of were 2 Corinthians 5:7 which reads: "For we live by faith, not by sight." And, Isaiah 41:10 reads: "So do not fear, for I am with you; do not be dismayed, for I am your God. I will strengthen you and help you; I will uphold you with my righteous right hand."

I realized that although I had to say goodbye to Horace and all my friends, Jesus would help me to hold on to my faith. And although buckets of tears were shed by all of us when we left, Jesus would be with me every step of the way. He would strengthen me and hold me in His hands.

During the five years my family spent at Woodfield

Park Baptist Church under the leadership of Rev. Horace B. Youngblood, we enjoyed a lifetime of fellowship. I learned the bulk of God's Word from him. Horace and Bennie will forever be friends I hold dear. They will forever be that part of my childhood when I learned the ways of the Christian faith.

Next, I share my story of Charles A. Sineath. I just learned of Charles' passing on July 23, 2022. I'm writing this on August 2, 2022. I'll stop here for a while as this has hit me hard. It will be a few days before I pick it up again. I'm in great need to have tea with Jesus. Philippians 1:3 "I thank my God every time I remember you."

Now, back to Charles. Born in Cordele, Georgia on March 29, 1939. Charles attended Duke University and then transferred to and graduated from Emory University. He then attended Emory's Candler School of Theology and graduated with a master's in theology. But it wasn't just his education or his master's degree that left me with good memories of him, it was his talent for delivering the Word of God. His knowledge of the Bible always amazed me. That and his love of people—especially his congregation.

Charles began his ministry in 1961. In 1973 he became the senior pastor at Marietta First United Methodist Church. My family came to know Charles as members of Marietta FUMC in 1977 a year after my husband and I were married. From that moment until we left Atlanta, we absorbed the sermons Charles poured out over his congregation. Charles spent twenty-six years at Marietta FUMC. He retired in 1999 from the North Georgia United Methodist Conference, but his ministry didn't end there. Charles went on to start the Wesleyan Fellowship, which is now known as Riverstone Church in Kennesaw, Georgia.

I remember when I first met Charles. When he spoke to you, he looked right into your eyes. I always loved that. He made you feel as though you were the most important person he'd ever met. Because of that, Charles always knew how his congregants were getting along.

When Charles stood at the pulpit you knew he would be speaking from the Bible. His sermons were rooted in scripture. His personal relationship with the Lord led him in every way, and he had no problem standing up for what he believed in. Ultimately, he paid the price for what he believed. He stood firm on his belief regarding homosexuality and the road on which the United Methodist Church seemed determined to travel down, even in 1999. And now, in the year 2022, the United Methodist Church is in disarray. The church punished Charles for his stance not only on homosexuality but other social issues as well. It broke my heart then. It breaks my heart still.

We moved to Texas in 1992 so we weren't in Atlanta in 1999 when it all went down. But be assured I would have been among the thousands who walked out of that church never to return on Charles' last day.

I came upon an article about Charles whereby a friend of his stated that Charles was willing to pay the price for what he believed. The minister of my mother's church (a Baptist church) made that statement. I never knew they were friends. But the part that impressed me the most about his full statement was when he visited with Charles on his last day as minister of Marietta FUMC. He's quoted as saying, "Charles, if when we walk out this door in a minute, Jesus Christ was standing there, he would say, 'Well done,' and we walked out together." What a testament of a true friend and a true believer in the word of God.

In 2002 Charles retired a second time. He came out of retirement to pastor at Mountain View Alliance Church from 2005 to 2010. He retired another time only to go back to the ministry he loved. He gave his last sermon three weeks before he passed.

Anyone who ever sat and listened to a sermon by Charles

will tell you that he ended his sermons with, "Good news, Good news, Good news," and proceeded to tell you why.

I will forever remember Charles as one of the two ministers in my life who left the biggest impression and taught me what it means to be a Christian.

Horace B. Youngblood and Charles A. Sineath both heard the call to minister. They accepted it and led their congregations according to the word of God. As I sat and had tea with Jesus over this story, He reminded me that the Bible speaks to leadership and its responsibilities as well as our responsibility as Christians to follow.

Hebrews 13:7 reads: "Remember your leaders, who spoke the word of God to you. Consider the outcome of their way of life and imitate their faith."

Jeremiah 3:15 reads: "Then I will give you shepherds after my own heart, who will lead you with knowledge and understanding."

Rest in peace Horace and Charles. You were not only my ministers, you were my friends. Until we meet again…

Perfume and incense bring joy to the heart, and the pleasantness of a friend springs from their heartfelt advice. Proverbs 27:9

35

That Time an Angel Rescued Our Daughter

Psalm 91:11-12 / Psalm 103:20

MY BELIEF IN ANGELS RUNS DEEP. I'VE SEEN WHAT HAPPENS when an angel intervenes. We were in the process of selling our house when our oldest daughter graduated from high school. My husband had already relocated while our girls and I stayed behind hoping the house would sell. Since our daughter had graduated, we thought it best for her to apply to college in our new town. She did and was accepted. School went well for a few months—and then she suddenly went missing.

She'd made friends with a girl and guy who, we were told, she'd met at school. My husband searched for her for months to no avail. Since she was considered an adult, we couldn't do much.

When the house finally sold, we were reunited with my husband, but our daughter had yet to be found. The only thing we knew was that her car had been repossessed. My husband finally located the apartment complex where she'd been living with this couple we thought she'd met at school. He had no luck finding her any of the times he went to the apartments.

I'd given up all hope we'd ever find her. I feared for her life, and every time the phone rang my heart sank.

I spent many hours writing in my journal and having tea with Jesus. He always reminded me of Psalm 91:11-12 which reads: "For he will command his angels concerning you to guard you in all your ways; they will lift you up in their hands, so that you will not strike your foot against a stone." Angels—I hadn't always believed in them. I'd read stories of their existence. I knew the Bible spoke of them. Their power, as spoken about in Psalm 103:20: "Praise the Lord, you his angels, you mighty ones who do his bidding, who obey his word." Still, I held on to my skepticism about their actual existence. Jesus knew this about me and continued to comfort me and encourage me to believe.

One night after many months of trying to track our daughter down, we heard a knock on the door. When we opened the door there she stood, shaking. She appeared sick. We wrapped our arms around her and wept.

We took her to the doctor the next day. He said she had a bladder infection and put her on some meds. After a few days had passed and the meds had kicked in, she felt better. We sat in the living room of our apartment and talked for several hours.

She poured out her heart about where she'd been. She'd met the couple not at school but at a party. They convinced her that she didn't need to go to school and to come live with them and they would show her how to make a lot of money. She fell for it. They then began to deplete her bank account. She started writing bad checks to the tune of over fifty thousand dollars. The majority she wrote herself, but some of the larger ones they forged her name.

They bounced around from apartment building to apartment building. That's why we could never find her. The day before the night she showed up at our apartment, she'd overheard them plotting to kill her. They didn't know she was in the apartment. When they left, she grabbed what things she had and ran.

I asked her how she'd gotten to our apartment. Who brought her? She said, "I didn't know him. He saw me walking and offered me a lift. The next thing I knew I was standing at your door. I turned to thank him and he wasn't there. He seemed to disappear."

"Do you remember what he looked like?" I asked.

"That's the weirdest part. The entire time I couldn't get a clear look at his face. And I don't think I would be able to describe him even if I had seen his face," she responded.

I reflected on the scripture Jesus reminded me of one of the times when we had tea over my distress of not finding our daughter. *He will give his angels charge of you to guard you in all your ways.* I know now Jesus tried to give me a message that our daughter would be protected and that she would return home.

Did Jesus send an angel to bring our daughter home? I will always believe He did. God created angels, so why wouldn't He send one to save our daughter? From the Bible, we know there are three types of angles. Cherubim, Seraphin, and living creatures. Only two angels have names; they are Gabriel and Michael. Angels are very powerful. They are also examples for us to follow. They are the perfect example of obedience. Angles model worship. Who better to bring our daughter back to us?

That nineteen-year-old girl is now fifty years old. She has a family. Three amazing kids (all grown). A great husband; they own a business together. The time she went missing seemed like it lasted for eons. The fear, the anger, the sadness, the tears. All the feelings going on at the same time. There were days I didn't think I could get out of bed. But I did. We moved forward. It took time for our daughter to get back to the normalcy of life. She'd hurt us all terribly. She'd hurt herself more.

When your child goes missing at the age that's considered

adulthood, you don't just feel helpless—you truly *are* helpless. Over the years, it's been difficult for her to forgive herself. We've had conversations about that. My husband and I forgave her even before she ever asked. Doesn't our Father in Heaven do the same for us? Her sisters took a little longer to get over it, but now it's as if it never happened. She's grown and matured into such an amazing woman, wife, mother, daughter, sister, and business owner.

The last time Jesus and I sat and had tea about my oldest daughter didn't happen right after she came home. Jesus and I have talked extensively about her throughout the years. I've fretted about her forgiveness of herself. I've explained to her many times that every member of our family forgave her years ago. I just don't see on her face that she's forgiven herself yet.

Jesus poured into my heart Romans 5:6–8 "You see, at just the right time, when we were still powerless, Christ died for the ungodly. Very rarely will anyone die for a righteous person, though for a good person someone might possibly dare to die. But God demonstrates his own love for us in this: While we were still sinners, Christ died for us." I believe this with all I have inside of me.

That time my daughter went missing is the time I fully understood that life can turn on a dime. It helped me to understand that our children, regardless of their age, will always be our children, and we must never shy away from expressing not only our dismay with them but also our love for them and forgiveness for things they do. Would not God do the same for us?

36

That Time the Churches Closed Their Doors

Romans 13:1-7 / Psalm 46

WE ALL WENT THROUGH THE HORRORS OF WATCHING THE doors of our churches close during the time in which we don't speak of (COVID-19) ravaged the world. I'll admit I got angry. "Oh, ye of little faith!" I got belligerent. I didn't like it one little bit. What were we thinking?

I get it, people were afraid. We were facing a virus we knew nothing about. No knowledge of how to treat it or beat it. No medication, procedure, or vaccine to deal with it. But it's my thought that when information is transmitted to the public that speaks at first to a small number of people infected, fear steps in. It multiplies and becomes a monster. From mask mandates, to social distancing, to vaccines, to shutdowns. The monster grew and grew until no one knew anything about anything. No one knew what to do. So they shut it all down.

I've read tons of material about the pros and cons of mask wearing. The pros and cons of getting the vaccine. Honestly, I'm so over it all. My biggest heartache came with not being able to go to church because the church doors were forced closed. And they stayed closed for well over a year.

About the only positive thing I can say is that at least we could view a sermon from my church online. Forgive me if that doesn't or didn't excite me. I missed sitting in church with my church family. I missed God's house so very much. But I stuck it out, taking time to have hundreds of teas with Jesus.

Jesus saw and felt my anger. He reminded me of Romans 13:1-7, which speaks to the submission to governing authorities: "Let everyone be subject to the governing authorities, for there is no authority except that which God has established. The authorities that exist have been established by God. Consequently, whoever rebels against the authority is rebelling against what God has instituted, and those who do so will bring judgment on themselves. For rulers hold no terror for those who do right, but for those who do wrong. Do you want to be free from fear of the one in authority? Then do what is right and you will be commended. For the one in authority is God's servant for your good. But if you do wrong, be afraid, for rulers do not bear the sword for no reason. They are God's servants, agents of wrath to bring punishment on the wrongdoer. Therefore, it is necessary to submit to the authorities, not only because of possible punishment but also as a matter of conscience. This is also why you pay taxes, for the authorities are God's servants, who give their full time to governing. Give to everyone what you owe them: If you owe taxes, pay taxes; if revenue, then revenue; if respect, then respect; if honor, then honor." I understood the reasoning behind this scripture, but Jesus knew my soul still ached. He knew I still harbored anger in my heart.

Honestly, I didn't want to stop being angry. As a human being and as an American, the fact that we are a free people offered me the freedom to express myself authentically in the world. There should be nothing done to me that I didn't give my consent. That included my freedom to worship in God's house. With doors closed and lockdowns in place, this demon called COVID-19 had curtailed my freedoms. And I felt it was all done in the name of societal health. Who gets to tell me I can't go to church? Who gets to make decisions on behalf of everyone? In the end, what did all that do to the people of America? This pandemic brought the world to a halt.

There's been so much we've learned since February of 2020. We now know how masks affected our kids. We also know if masks worked at all. We know more about the vaccine that we were all either urged or pressured into taking. We've discovered how immunities work. We also know if social distancing helps. If I had to pick something good that's come out of this beast, I'd have to say that it made many of us appreciate our freedoms more. Some families became closer. Innovation went wild. As Christians, we probably prayed more. Parents discovered it's not so easy being a teacher. But they also learned who the bad apples were in education. Overall, it became a learning experience for us all and hopefully taught us not to continue making the same mistakes.

As I sat and had tea with Jesus toward the end (kinda / sorta end) of the pandemic, still a bit raw from it all, Jesus offered me Psalm 46. He reminded me that He is my strength and my refuge. He helps me in times of trouble. I should never fear, even if the earth gave way and all the mountains fell into the sea. Most of all Jesus said, "Be still, and know that I am God." Jesus also reminded me of the last passage of Psalm 46 that reads: "The Lord Almighty is with us; The God of Jacob is our fortress." I felt much better.

37

That Time My Papa Saw My Grandma— But Grandma Died Years Before

Mark 10:9

MY PAPA LOVED MY GRANDMA LIKE NO OTHER. HE ADORED her. They were precious together. He took it upon himself to be her protector, never allowing anything to hurt her—or so he thought. In all their years together, he believed he could protect her until the end of time. He felt he could protect her against anything life could and would throw at them. But he was wrong.

None of us have the power to combat all illnesses. Of course, there are doctors. Specialists, even. But there are some diseases doctors can't cure no matter how hard they try. You see, my grandma suffered from severe diabetes for many years. Diabetes took away the toes on her feet. It took away her ability to walk. It sent her into convulsions. Most egregious, it slowly started taking away her eyesight. It became a monster that fed off the doses of insulin at an astonishing rate.

My papa was ill-equipped to take care of her. It hurt his heart so much to see how the evils of diabetes affected her tiny body. So while my uncle Buck took care of Grandma's physical needs, Papa cared for her in the way a husband cares for his wife. He sat with her and read to her. They shared many conversations about their life together and the twelve kids they'd made and raised and saw pass on before them.

At the age of sixty-nine, on July 24, 1961, diabetes won. It took my grandma's life. I think we all died a little that day. Hattie Oxendine Bell born January 21, 1892, shone like the light in the children's song, "This Little Light of Mine." I knew even as a child the impact my grandma's death would have on my papa.

After Grandma passed, Papa seemed to roam aimlessly. His face never again lit with the love of seeing Grandma walk into a room. Sadness took him over and shook him for all its worth. The family stepped up making sure Papa never felt alone. But still, he did. Regardless of how much we all tried to alleviate his pain, we couldn't.

I spent many tea times with Jesus asking how I might help. Jesus told me that Papa and Grandma were that couple who stayed together for life. They loved each other so much. Death would not change that. He reminded me of Mark 10:9 which reads: "Therefore what God has joined together, let no one separate." In their hearts, they would never be apart.

Years passed, as they always do, and Papa found himself able to face the mornings. He told me that he still missed Grandma so much. If he could just see her beautiful face one more time, he'd be happy. I told him maybe he should have tea with Jesus.

I remember being in my early twenties and on one of my visits to North Carolina when Papa told me a story. He had to sell his house and move in with his daughter, my Aunt Sarah. He couldn't get along by himself and needed help in almost everything. Aunt Sarah made the perfect caregiver. They got along great. Plus she was the bossy pants of the entire family. Everyone did what she said to avoid the Aunt Sarah smack down. I always thought Papa made out pretty well as Aunt Sarah was a stinkin' good cook. He seemed happy there, and that's what mattered most.

On this one particular visit he asked, "Remember when I told you if I could only see your grandma one more time, I'd be happy?"

"Yes," I responded, quite curiously.

"Well, the other night…I saw her," he said, eyes dancing around in his head.

"What do you mean you saw her? You know Grandma is dead, right?" I asked.

"Of course, I know that, child. I'm old. I'm not senile," he snapped.

"So what do you mean you saw her if you know she's dead, Papa?" I asked.

"The other night I couldn't sleep," he began. "I tossed and turned until I finally I propped my pillow up and sat up in the bed. I thought I might read a bit from the Good Book. That always seems to calm me. I was reading 2 Corinthians 4:18—*So we fix our eyes not on what is seen, but on what is unseen, since what is seen is temporary, but what is unseen is eternal.* I looked up and there sat your grandma, child. She was all aglow. Her long hair hung down around her shoulders. I couldn't keep my eyes off her. She was so beautiful. So beautiful. I reached out to touch her, but she shook her head no. I guess it wasn't my time to go be with her. Just as suddenly as she appeared, she disappeared. It was the most precious time of my life, child."

There were tears in my papa's eyes. I'd never once seen my papa cry. In that moment I realized just how much he loved Grandma. It was the most precious time of *my* life. Jesus was right. Even death couldn't separate them from their love.

On June 2, 1976, my papa, Luther James Bell, died—fifteen years after the love of his life, Hattie, died. There's not a doubt in my mind that he and Grandma are together again. I can see them walking along the shore of the Jordan hand in hand.

"Therefore what God has joined together, let no one separate."

38

That Time I Went to the 1969 Atlanta International Pop Festival

Proverbs 12:19 / Exodus 20:12 / Philippians 3:13

WHY IS IT THAT WHEN WE ARE YOUNG, ESPECIALLY IN our teen years, we think we are invincible? I'm sure it's been that way since the beginning of time. For those of us who remember Woodstock—you know, the one held in New York in 1969? Coined "3 Days of Peace and Music." Held on Max Yasgur's dairy farm in Bethel, New York. Approximately 400,000 peeps showed up. Thirty-two acts performed. Everything happened outside rain or shine. And it did rain sporadically. Well, I didn't go to that one. I did, however, go to what we now fondly call the "Baby Woodstock" held July 4-5, 1969. This one went down about a month before the famous Woodstock in New York.

The Atlanta International Pop Festival, held at the Atlanta International Raceway in Hampton, Georgia, was the first festival of its kind in Atlanta. About 150,000 peeps showed up to that one, and I was among that crowd. Unbeknownst to my parents, of course, who would have lost their minds and chained me to the pole in our basement for the remainder of my life.

My adventure began when one of my friends wanted to introduce me to this guy she knew. A friend of her boyfriend's, she said. They were planning a trip to the Atlanta International Pop Festival and he needed a date. He's such a great guy, she said. You'll love him, she said. He's in the military, she said.

Now at the time, I had just recently turned seventeen, so I knew this guy had to be in his twenties if he was in the military. Note: the following is how a just recently turned seventeen-year-old girl's brain works. Out of those three truly informative things my friend told me about this guy the only question I asked was "Is he cute?" Her response—"Would I be fixing you up with him if he wasn't? He's in the military for crying out loud. Those guys are buff!" Upon meeting him— yes, he had the buffness going on and the cuteness on top of that.

With the lie told to my parents, my friend, her boyfriend, the buff/cute military guy, and I were on our way to the Atlanta International Pop Festival, and ready to party. You're wondering what about tea with Jesus right about now, aren't you? Nope. Didn't happen. Not then. Tea with Jesus couldn't have been further from my mind. All I saw was the lineup of acts I'd read about in the paper:

(July 4–5, 1969-Line up: underlined performed at the Woodstock in New York: Chuck Berry, Al Kooper, <u>Blood, Sweat & Tears</u>, Booker T & the MGs, <u>Canned Heat</u>, Chicago Transit Authority, <u>Creedence Clearwater Revival</u>, Dave Brubeck, Delaney, Bonnie & Friends, Ian & Sylvia, Grand Funk Railroad, <u>Janis Joplin</u>, <u>Johnny Winter</u>, Led Zeppelin, Pacific Gas & Electric, <u>Paul Butterfield Blues Band</u>, Johnny Rivers, Spirit, <u>Sweetwater</u>, and Ten Wheel Drive)

Now I ask you, if you were a recently turned seventeen-year-old, would you, too, not lie to your parents to have a chance to see these people perform? For me, the fact that I'd be seeing Janis Joplin made whatever punishment I might receive, should my parents discover where I'd been, totally worth it.

When we arrived at the Atlanta International Raceway in Hampton, Georgia, my eyes glazed over. I'd never seen that many people in one place. Traffic was backed up for miles. Did I mention the temperatures hit about one hundred degrees? The city called in the local fire departments so they could use their fire hoses to create sprinklers for everyone to run around in and cool off. Some kind soul even brought in a truckload of watermelons to give out to the people. Watermelon rinds were everywhere. But it didn't matter. I don't even remember what, if anything, I ate all day. The entire thing was mesmerizing.

I remember they did sell t-shirts, but alas, I never got one. I'm sure if I had it would be worth a lot of money today. As I looked across the crowd of people I saw makeshift tents, people laying on blankets or towels, hundreds of coolers, lounge chairs, and girls sitting atop their boyfriend's shoulders. They had concession stands, but they were inadequate for the number of people. You could wait an hour just to get a soda.

There were drugs everywhere. You could smell them in the air. I remember it scared me a bit since I only pretended to be a hippie and had never once done drugs. But, hey, my date happened to be the buff/cute military guy, and I knew he'd protect me, even if we'd only known one another for a few hours.

The governing powers in Atlanta never wanted this festival in their city. They believed it would bring in all sorts of hippie-types from all over who would corrupt the youth of the South. Never mind that Sixteenth Street in Atlanta already shared its space with hundreds of hippies. My parents never allowed me to venture to Sixteenth Street. Yet I took it upon myself to travel with a guy I'd just met to Hampton, Georgia, to the first Atlanta International Pop Festival. I'm sure Jesus just shook His head at that as He sat patiently waiting for our tea time together, because He knew I'd show up eventually.

Remarkably the festival had very few incidents. One thing blew my mind though. Before I die, I must put it out there that while attending the 1969 Atlanta International Pop Festival I saw a naked man for the first time in my life. I knew at that very moment, regardless of whether my parents found out about this road trip or not, having tea with Jesus topped my list of things to do when I got home. But honestly, although the naked man unnerved me, I felt bad about deceiving my parents. It wasn't something I normally did. Well, maybe not every single day.

This festival appeared in every newspaper in Atlanta. They knew about it. They shared the same feelings as most parents. Teens my age weren't ready to experience anything like this. Especially a just recently turned seventeen-year-old who'd never been in a crowd that large, much less that type of crowd with a buff/cute military guy.

When I returned home, I didn't hesitate to make a tea time with Jesus. How many times had Jesus reminded me of Proverbs 12:19 which speaks to lying? "Truthful lips endure forever, but a lying tongue lasts only a moment." Or Exodus 20:12 which reads: "Honor your father and your mother, so that you may live long in the land the Lord your God is giving you." He knew at this moment my tea time with Him revolved around regret. He shared with me Philippians 3:13

which reads: "Brothers and sisters, I do not consider myself yet to have taken hold of it. But one thing I do: Forgetting what is behind and straining toward what is ahead." He wanted me to know that He never wanted me to grieve over past mistakes or have regrets. Dwelling in the past or focusing on regrets never allows us to do all the amazing things He has planned for us. Jesus said that my past would always follow me. And so, it has.

The 1969 Atlanta International Pop Festival is a day I *will* remember for the rest of my life. The sights, the sounds, the smells, and the music. Even the naked man.

39

That Time I Tried to Shave My Legs for the First Time in the Sink

Romans 1:22 / Proverbs 28:26

STUPIDITY COMES IN ALL SIZES. FOR ME, MY TEENS WERE MY MOST stupid years. At the age of thirteen—the beginning of my utter stupidity—I decided the time had arrived for me to shave my legs. All my friends shaved their legs. Why not me? Never mind that I had not one hair on my legs. It just seemed the appropriate time to begin this adult woman ritual.

Had I told my mother my thoughts on shaving my legs she most likely would have said, "Are you out of your mind? You're only thirteen. No!" So why tell her, right?

Now I've read several articles on the subject of "at what age should girls start shaving their legs." Many of them say the same thing. When girls hit puberty is when they want to start shaving their legs. I'm pretty sure at thirteen that's what made me want to start shaving my legs—puberty. Then these articles go on to say that in today's world puberty can begin as early as eight. However, for the most part, it does typically begin between the ages of ten and fourteen.

I read how puberty can cause the hair on your legs to become coarse and more noticeable and, consequently, the kids at school might start making fun of your child. The authors of these articles recommend talking to your daughter and dealing with confidence and self-esteem before you start talking to her about shaving. Okay, so that's fair enough. But then they turn right back around and say there's no harm in starting to shave early. But then! These same authors tell you to make sure your kid can handle a razor responsibly and shaving regularly once she starts shaving—wait, what? To top it all off, these articles end by stating that ultimately there's no right or wrong age for your daughter to start shaving her legs. Then why did I spend all this time reading your stupid article in the first place?

For the first time in my life, I find myself agreeing with my mother. "Are you out of your mind? You're only thirteen. No!" In 1968 (the year I turned thirteen), that's how it went down. Mothers didn't consult other people. They made their own decisions for their kids. Okay, so maybe some of them were actually reading Dr. Spock. But my mother? Not a chance. She stood firm and confident in the role of motherhood.

Knowing my mother would never allow me to shave my legs, I took it upon myself to do it anyway. I needed a plan, though. It had to happen when my parents were gone. I couldn't even have one of my friends over. This had to be something I did alone. So, I waited.

Finally, one Saturday afternoon, my parents said they had to run a couple of errands but wouldn't be gone long. As I waved goodbye from the driveway, my excitement about my brilliant plan grew. I waited until I couldn't see their car any longer as they drove away down the road. Then I ran inside and prepared to become a woman!

I gathered all the items I needed. Daddy's shaving cream—check. Daddy's razor—check. Washcloth and towel—check. Bar of soap—check. I walked into the bathroom and closed the door. After turning on the faucet, I put the razor and shaving cream on the counter along with the towel and washcloth. I made sure the water was warm. My friends had told me that part.

Now I must stop here to share some math and some logic. Sinks or lavatories, however one wants to call them, are meant to wash one's hands or face. I'm pretty sure they were not made for people to shave their legs in. That's the logic. As for the math—most sinks in the 1960s, not unlike today, are anywhere between 32" – 36" tall. Our sink most likely hit the 36" height mark. The average height of a thirteen-year-old is right at 5 feet. I'm only 5'2" as an adult so at age thirteen, I couldn't have been more than 4 feet, maybe even less. If the sink measured 36" (that's 3 feet) and I measured 4 feet, how easy or *difficult* would it be to get my leg up and over the edge of the sink and into the running water without wobbling? Pretty dang difficult, I'd say, based on the math.

Back to the "all my friends are shaving their legs" story. As I raised my right leg up and over the edge of the sink, my left leg wabbling, I splashed the water all over my leg making sure I got it nice and wet. I washed it with the bar of soap as per my friends' instructions. Don't ask why. I reached over to get my daddy's shaving cream with my leg all wet, soaped up, and slippery. In a split second...KAPOW! My left leg slipped out from under me, my right leg all wet, soaped up and slippery had no friction due to the water and soap. I came down hard, my chin hitting the edge of the sink. As I hit the floor, I grabbed my chin with my hand. When I pulled my hand away blood ran everywhere.

I'll never know why my parents came home from running their errands earlier than they anticipated, but right at the moment I fell, saw the blood, and started to scream, they walked in the door and heard my commotion. They ran to the bathroom screaming my name and found me on the floor, blood everywhere. I ended up in the ER and came home with five stitches on my chin.

To my surprise, my parents didn't reprimand me, deciding the five stitches were punishment enough. I did confess to what I'd tried to do. My mother just shook her head and said, "Try not to grow up too fast. And at least wait until you have some hair on your legs to shave. We can talk about the right way to go about it at that time."

My daddy, well, he just left the room. Talking about girl stuff made him nervous.

That night as I sat and had tea with Jesus, He talked with me about making wise decisions instead of foolish ones. He brought up Romans 1:22 which reads: "Although they claimed to be wise, they became fools."

"It's easy to fall into the pond of foolishness," Jesus said.

"Yeah, I do feel pretty foolish," I responded.

"As long as you acknowledge your mistakes and trust more in your parents' wisdom, I know you will make better choices in the future," Jesus said in His ever-comforting way.

Before our tea ended, Jesus showed me one more scripture. He wanted me to go away with one more instruction. He pointed to Proverbs 28:26 which reads: "Those who trust in themselves are fools, but those who walk in wisdom are kept safe."

I got the feeling that He had a hand in bringing my parents home at just the right time. It all could have been a lot worse. I guess timing is everything and there's a time for everything. Even shaving your legs.

40

That Time I Saw Pearl Harbor

James 4:1-2

ISTORY NEVER INTERESTED ME AT ALL IN MY YOUNGER YEARS. In high school, I hated every second of U.S. and World History. Now I find it quite interesting. Take, for instance, Pearl Harbor. In high school when we studied America's involvement in World War II, I all but fell asleep in class. There's something about aging that makes one appreciate history. I find myself wanting to know more. Not only about my country, the United States of America, but the world around me as well.

In 1997 my middle daughter graduated from high school. As a graduation gift, my husband and I gave her a trip to Hawaii. We decided the entire family would share in her good fortune. So we flew to Hawaii, staying the majority of our trip in Kauai. We had the best time. Kauai is so very lovely.

On our return part of the trip, we stayed in Honolulu. Not as lovely as Kauai and a lot more crowded. We did, however, have the opportunity to see the filming of the TV series *Baywatch*. Fun, but then our attention turned toward Oahu, Hawaii, which is west of Honolulu, the location of Pearl Harbor.

Naval fleets from the U.S. visited Pearl Harbor. In 1875, the U.S. acquired what's known as the Hawaiian Kingdom, made possible by the signing of the Reciprocity Treaty. As you look around Pearl Harbor now, you'll see it's a U.S. Navy deep-water base as well as the headquarters of the United States Pacific Fleet.

The history behind Pearl Harbor looks like this: December 7, 1941, a day when the soldiers thought they were going to get a little rest, Japan thought otherwise. At 7:55 a.m. Hawaii time, Japanese fighter planes attacked the United States Pacific Fleet without warning. Three hundred and sixty Japanese warplanes swarmed down like locusts. The U.S. had stayed silent about the war going on in Europe. Roosevelt ignored the warnings of Churchill, whose country found itself neck-deep in a war with Hitler. So when Japan attacked Pearl Harbor, Roosevelt could ignore it no longer. The U.S. joined World War II.

When we arrived at Pearl Harbor, we were in awe of what we saw. During the attack, a good part of the Pacific fleet was rendered useless. As we walked around the area, we stopped to read the information provided.

Some stats we learned: 5 out of 8 battleships, 3 destroyers, and 7 other ships were sunk or catastrophically damaged. Over 200 aircraft were destroyed. There were a total of 2,400 Americans killed. 1,200 were wounded. The soldiers on the ground tried valiantly to retaliate. The Japanese lost about 30 planes and approximately five midget subs. They lost fewer than 100 men. It took only two hours for the Japanese to accomplish what they thought would be their opportunity to control the pacific.

The mastermind behind the attack? Admiral Isoroku Yamamoto. He didn't want to attack Pearl Harbor. He didn't want this fight with America. But since Japan was part of WWII already, he needed the oil that certain countries possessed located in southeastern Asia. Pearl Harbor seemed his best bet due to its location to these countries. So he decided to go ahead with the surprise attack. Unfortunately for him, he "awoke a sleeping giant."

Six months later, the three Pacific fleet carriers that weren't docked at Pearl Harbor during the attack had their revenge. The Battle of Midway will be remembered as that time the tide turned and the U.S. came away with a spectacular victory.

Most of us remember from history class (even me) Roosevelt's speech before a joint session of Congress when he exclaimed, "Yesterday, December 7, 1941-a date which will live in infamy—the United States of America was suddenly and deliberately attacked by naval and air forces of the Empire of Japan." Congress approved the resolution to go to war with Japan and the rest, as they say, is history.

The Pearl Harbor National Monument is built on the water above the wreckage of the U.S.S. Arizona. Constructed in 1962, millions of people visit it on an annual basis. Before we boarded the U.S. Navy boat to cross over to the Monument, we saw a 23-minute documentary film about the attack on Pearl Harbor. We then took the boat to the Monument. It's a self-guided tour. You could rent a one-hour audio presentation. We didn't. Visitors are asked to remain silent as they tour the Monument. In all my life I've never been so moved by what I saw. You can see the U.S.S. Arizona and U.S.S. Utah that are still on the bottom of Pearl Harbor. What's so gut-wrenching is that the soldiers' bodies are still inside these ships. Another part of our visit that tore at our hearts was seeing the top part of the U.S.S. Arizona. You can see oil leaking from this part of the ship. They call it "the tears of the Arizona."

My trip to the Pearl Harbor National Monument wore me down. Our visit back to a time when war was raging and people were being murdered by a madman in Germany and a warmonger who wanted to cripple the U.S. left me crying buckets.

I felt inadequate as a human being learning about all the heroics that went on that day.

As I sat with Jesus having a much-needed tea time with Him, I asked Him how people hate like that. Where does that kind of hate come from? Why do countries feel they need to war against one another? Jesus simply reminded me of James 4:1-2 which reads: "What causes fights and quarrels among you? Don't they come from your desires that battle within you? You desire but do not have, so you kill. You covet but you cannot get what you want, so you quarrel and fight. You do not have because you do not ask God." So that's it? Yes, that's it. When we battle within ourselves, anger pours out of us. Sometimes over nothing. Wars happen for this very reason—we desire but we do not have, so we kill. Jesus wanted me to understand that one fact. He wanted me to know why coveting is so bad.

Pearl Harbor became the recipient of hatred and coveting. Because of these two things, thousands of lives were lost. I'll never forget my visit to Pearl Harbor, a time when I learned the meaning of sacrifice.

41

That Time I Lost My Senior Ring in The Ocean

Luke Chapter 15 / 2 Peter 3:9 / Psalm 32

M Y SENIOR YEAR OF HIGH SCHOOL. OH THE MEMORIES. BEST year of my entire educational career. I'd made the Drill Team and attended drill team camp that summer. Our name—The Therrell High Hi-Steppers. I couldn't have been more proud of myself for being a part of one of the most popular groups. I sported a new hairdo that year. My skin glowed with a dark tan that all my friends envied. My senior pictures came out great. I'd ordered my announcements—*Look at me! I'm a Senior! Yay Class of 1970!* I'd ordered my cap and gown. More importantly, my senior ring arrived at the end of my junior year. I put it on my finger the moment I received it and vowed to never take it off. Life seemed perfect.

The summer before my senior year began a friend asked if I'd like to join her and her parents on a trip to Panama City, Florida. Of course, I said yes. Drill Team Camp didn't begin for another month. My friend and I were so excited we didn't sleep a wink the night before we left. I loved Panama City. I'd been there several times with my parents.

When we arrived at the beach, my friend, Susan, and I

changed into our swimsuits the moment we got to our room. Grabbing our baby oil laced with iodine, our towels, and our transistor radios, we headed for the beach. Now I know what caught your eye—it's the baby oil laced with iodine. We indeed smeared it all over our bodies. Supposedly it prevented you from burning as we baked ourselves in the sun. But, hey, we were the kids who drank from garden hoses. No fear whatsoever.

As we sat baking ourselves, we drew the attention of a couple of guys. They moseyed on over and introduced themselves. We allowed them to linger a bit for one reason only. They were drop-dead cute. After a while of teenage talking, the guys asked us out. We, of course, accepted. I mean who wouldn't accept a date from a couple of hunks? Why would it even matter that we had no idea who these guys were? They might have been serial killers or rapists. Or human traffickers. Too bad the movie *Taken* hadn't come out yet. We might not have made the date. But, hey, we were the teens of 1969, the year of the hippies, peace, and love. Plus when you're a teen, you're invincible.

We met the guys after Susan's parents were asleep. We had adjoining rooms at the hotel so it was easy enough. The guys told us they would meet us on the beach in front of our hotel at 10:00 p.m.

In the beginning, everything went fine. They took us to a beach house where they were staying with a group of guys. The alcohol flowed, and Susan and I drank too much. Some of the guys made advances. To their credit, the guys we came with defended our honor. Seeing just how drunk we were, the guys took us back to our hotel and helped us get to our room. I have no idea how we didn't wake Susan's parents, but we didn't. The next morning, we were miserable.

As I got into the shower, I noticed my senior ring was missing. I gasped and then began to panic. My friend heard me saying, loudly, "Where's my ring? My ring! Where's my ring?"

She came rushing into the bathroom asking if I was okay. Clearly not. My senior ring was gone. I started crying. How could I have lost my ring? Where could it possibly be? Then it hit me. I must have lost it on the beach with those guys. I knew in my heart of hearts I'd never find it. It had probably already washed out into the ocean. How would I ever explain to my parents that I'd lost my senior ring?

As I sat with my friend on the beach that afternoon I prayed my ring would just wash up on the shore right where we sat. Of course, it didn't. My friend asked if I had any savings from babysitting. I shook my head yes. Then, as if the same thought came into both of our heads at the same time, we said in unison, *Order another one!* My parents would never have to know—ever. And, that's exactly what I did. I ordered another senior ring. When it arrived, it didn't look as nice as my original ring. It looked cheaper somehow. Well, no need to fret. My parents wouldn't be able to notice the difference. All I needed to do was to stay calm. Go on with my life, never saying a word.

This time I heard *Jesus* calling me for tea time. I soon realized that He needed me to understand the meaning of possessions and how they can affect our judgment. He pointed me to Luke 15. This scripture is when Jesus tells a series of three parables. They all speak about possessions that were lost by their owners.

First, there's "The Parable of the Lost Sheep." Realizing he's missing one of his flock the shepherd walks away from all the other sheep to go and find that one. Then there's "The Parable of the Lost Coin." This one involved a woman who by whatever means has lost her entire day's pay. She begins frantically searching for her coins. Finally, there's "The Parable of the Lost Son." A kid who goes off the deep end with his inheritance only to realize there's no place like home.

I didn't understand at first what Jesus wanted me to get out of these parables since each story has a happy type ending in which they find what's lost. I knew I'd never find my ring. Jesus explained that although my ring was lost it belonged to me for a while. Just like sometimes people are lost but they belonged to God from the beginning. As people, we must look for God if we're to be saved. But in essence, it's God who never stops searching for us. If we look at 2 Peter 3:9 we read: "The Lord is not slow in keeping his promise, as some understand slowness. Instead he is patient with you, not wanting anyone to perish, but everyone to come to repentance."

Jesus reminded me that when we are lost and then found there is great rejoicing in heaven. From our being found, we will know eternal life. We will live with Him in His kingdom. That seemed to me to be the better outcome. Possessions should never become so important that we find ourselves doing things we shouldn't. The ring suddenly seemed less important.

"Tea time isn't over," Jesus said. "It's time to talk about deception and drinking."

I knew the drinking part was bad, particularly at my age. But I did it anyway, and I was ashamed.

Jesus said, "Our Father commands us as Christians that we should avoid drunkenness. However, you are a child, and drinking, for your age, is illegal. You do realize this, I'm sure. Understand something in this regard. Although the Bible does not speak to underage drinking, it does speak to obeying the law. Disobeying the law is disobeying God. I know you will think twice should you ever find yourself in a situation where alcohol is present."

I shook my head, yes, and promised Jesus I'd never allow something like that to happen again. I'm proud to say I never did.

Jesus then went on to the topic of deception. I confessed that I thought of deceiving my parents about my lost ring. I not only thought about it, I told myself I had no choice but to deceive them. It's that *what harm can it do* thing. If they knew I'd lost my ring, they'd be sad. I'd be sad because I knew a huge punishment would be coming my way. So why make us all miserable? But Jesus interjected with Genesis 3:1-15. The scene from the Garden of Eden. Adam and Eve tried to deceive God. Deceiving someone is the same as lying. Honesty is part of the Ten Commandments. Deception is always found out. Lies never stay lies forever.

Jesus made me realize that my deception would ruin my relationship with my parents. Should they ever discover I lost my senior ring in the ocean and then covered it up, what would that do to my relationship with them? They'd never trust me again. Even if I might be telling the truth, they wouldn't believe me. And who'd blame them?

I made a promise to Jesus that I would come clean to my parents about the ring. He left me with Psalm 32. The first two verses of that chapter are magnificent. It reads: "Blessed is the one whose transgressions are forgiven, whose sins are covered. Blessed is the one whose sin the Lord does not count against them and in whose spirit is no deceit."

It turned out that tea with Jesus led me to tell my parents about the ring. I even told them about buying another one to cover it up. They asked to see it and saw exactly what I saw. It wasn't as nice as my original ring which, most likely now sat in the belly of some enormous shark. I hope whoever that shark is he got indigestion.

42

That Time I Was a Waitress in My Daddy's Restaurant

Mark 10:45 / Hebrews 13:2 / 1 Peter 4:9

COULD THERE BE A MORE UNAPPRECIATED PROFESSION THAN that of a waitress? Well, maybe a teacher. Then there are mothers. Then there are police officers and firemen. What about the guys who pick up our trash? Wait! I'm sure there's more. But for this story, I'll be dealing with the job of a waitress. (Note: I'm using the word waitress fully aware of what I'm conveying. I'm female and females, in my world, are referred to as waitresses. Males are referred to as waiters.) Stick with me here.

My daddy owned a restaurant in the 1970s. He was an amazing chef. I've written about him before. This story, however, is about me. Daddy named his restaurant The Dellcliff. It sat right outside of Helen, Georgia. After being in the Army (Ret.) and then teaching (Ret.), my daddy decided he wanted to open a restaurant. Personally, I thought he'd lost his mind. The restaurant business is a killer. It's like farming. You have no day of rest. It's 24/7 365. But my daddy loved every second of it.

He and my mother bought some land in the town of Hiawassee, Georgia, which is on the other side of the mountain from the town of Helen. Then they purchased a mobile home and plopped it down in the middle of that land. Daddy had his eye on this one restaurant located at the far end of Helen, Georgia, for a while. So after they settled into their home, he approached the owner and made the deal. He renamed the restaurant The Dellcliff.

Daddy became not only the owner but the head chef. I'm pretty sure he felt like he'd died and gone to heaven. He was now living his dream. I decided it might be fun to drive to Helen on the weekends and help the waitstaff. My oldest daughter, Sandi, was about eight months old at the time, and I always took her with me. Daddy would put her in a high chair and sit it at the end of the bar so she could see everything going on around her. She loved it.

On Sundays, Daddy put on a lunch buffet that became not only the talk of the town of Helen but the talk of Georgia. People would drive in from all over the state to partake of Daddy's delicious food. We were all very proud of him.

As I donned my waitress uniform (yes, Daddy insisted on uniforms—old school thinking) and began my part-time career as a waitress, my view of human beings changed drastically. I discovered that people are pigs. No, make that rude and obnoxious pigs. Over the course of the next several years, I couldn't imagine choosing waitressing as a career. I soon developed the opinion that waitresses and waiters are angels sent down to earth by God to endure the overall disgusting actions of humans.

The one item I could possibly put into the pro column is that when you're a waitress you learn patience and humbleness. Neither has ever been one of my virtues. I had visions of pouring hot coffee into people's laps or dumping their entire plate of food on top of their heads. Some days were so full of hideous human beings that I even envisioned spitting in their iced tea. But I never did any of that. Daddy would have been none too happy. Trust me, no one in their right mind would want my daddy to be unhappy with them.

There were many times tea with Jesus became a time for me to tamp down my dark side. Jesus, always the comforter—always the challenger—never let me down by getting me to see things His way. He reminded me of three specific scriptures. Mark 10:45, Hebrews 13:2, and 1 Peter 4:9.

Jesus said, "Do you remember who I am? I am the Son of Man. Do you remember why my Father sent me?"

He pointed me to Mark 10:45: "For even the Son of Man did not come to be served, but to serve, and to give his life as a ransom for many." That one hit me hard.

Then Jesus brought up Hebrews 13:2: "Do not forget to show hospitality to strangers, for by so doing some people have shown hospitality to angels without knowing it." Okay, so I admit I took some issue with this. These people I'd waited on were *not* angels.

Jesus said, "And how do you know this? Have you seen their souls? Do you know their life history? Granted, some people are quite the challenge—even for Me. But you've said you want to see things (and people) as I do. Has that changed?"

Where does one go from there? I had to agree. There's a great Native American Proverb that goes like this: "Never judge another man until you have walked a mile in his moccasins."

Jesus took it a step further and put forth 1 Peter 4:9: "Offer hospitality to one another without grumbling." I get it. If I volunteered for this, I needed to be humble. I needed to serve and offer hospitality without the grumbling. Daddy never demanded or even asked for my help. I offered it freely.

I came away from this experience not only better for it but also with a higher respect for those who serve us at restaurants—waitresses and waiters alike. I will admit, however, that when I see a rude or obnoxious person in a restaurant, I do have the urge to pour hot coffee in their lap.

Jesus is shaking his head, isn't He?

Although this is the end of this book, it is not and never will be the end of my teas with Jesus.

Until we meet again, I bid you farewell.
In the meantime, I wish you a forever
walk with the Lord and when the
situation presents itself your personal
Tea with Jesus.

www.ingramcontent.com/pod-product-compliance
Lightning Source LLC
LaVergne TN
LVHW041319080426
835513LV00008B/516